JOURNEYS HA

'Like pilgrims to the appointed place we tend;
The worlds an inn and death the journey's end.'

Paloman and Arcite
John Dryden
1631 - 1700

To Elizabeth, Jocasta and Charlotte:
Three very special ladies

The author as OC
Support Company 1965

Journeys Hazardous

Gurkha clandestine operations

Borneo 1965

Christopher Bullock

A GURKHA MUSEUM PUBLICATION

First published in 1994 by
Square One Publications

Fourth Edition published in 2007

© The Gurkha Museum 2007

British Library Cataloguing in Publication Data
is available for this book

ISBN 978-0-9521487-1-5

Printed by Salisbury Printing Company Ltd
Greencroft Street, Salisbury, Wiltshire SP1 1JF

Contents

List of Maps

SOUTH-EAST ASIA

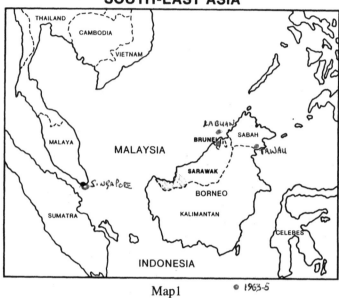

Map1

⊙ 1963-5

BORNEO FIRST DIVISION

Map2

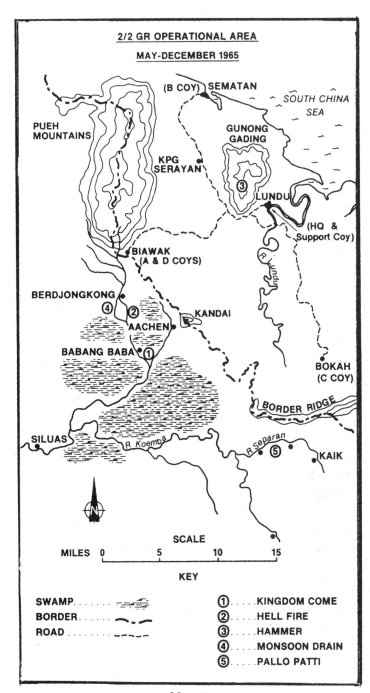

2/2 GR OPERATIONAL AREA
MAY-DECEMBER 1965

(B COY) SEMATAN

SOUTH CHINA SEA

PUEH MOUNTAINS

GUNONG GADING

KPG SERAYAN

③

LUNDU

(HQ & Support Coy)

R. Lundu

BIAWAK (A & D COYS)

BERDJONGKONG

④ ② KANDAI

AACHEN

BABANG BABA ①

BOKAH (C COY)

BORDER RIDGE

SILUAS

R. Koemba

R. Separan

⑤ KAIK

N

SCALE

MILES 0   5   10   15

KEY

SWAMP.	① . . . . KINGDOM COME
BORDER	② . . . . . HELL FIRE
ROAD	③ . . . . HAMMER
	④ . . . . . MONSOON DRAIN
	⑤ . . . . PALLO PATTI

Map 3

Introduction

This book tells of operations launched by Support Company 2nd Battalion 2nd KEO Gurkha Rifles between August and December 1965 against the Indonesian Army lines of communication in Indonesia. As the Company Commander I kept a diary of all that took place which was probably quite wrong since at that time the operations were politically extremely sensitive. As a result the diary lay collecting dust for twenty or so years until all the closely guarded secrets were released elsewhere. This book based on the diary is a young officer's tale and as such I am only too aware of its imperfections if read as anything other than a personal account. It records the operations we undertook and reactions to events by a twenty-four year old who had never been in action before Borneo. It is not therefore a book for those who seek knowledge of the campaign in overall strategy or political importance. Quite the contrary, its events only portray life at the sharp end and in themselves reflect a multitude of similar little struggles spread over the eight hundred mile border between Borneo and Indonesian

Kalimantan. Re-reading the diary I become conscious again not only of the naivety and foolhardiness, but also the romantic idealism that withers with oncoming age. One can now be very cynical about what seemed of such moment, but that very cynicism is dispelled by the blurred lines of faded writing smudged by sweat and mosquito oil. For these words tell of the matrix of low level conflict which made Britain's final success possible in an area where both time and space were against her.

This was a war not of Britain's seeking, indeed quite the contrary since she wished to shed her open-ended and expensive commitment in the Far East as expeditiously as possible.

By 1962 it became clear that General Soekarno of Indonesia had grandiose plans for much of South East Asia. He already had a name 'MAPHILINDO'; Malaysia, Philippines and Indonesia. It was with his support that the Brunei revolt was instigated aimed at removing the autocratic Sultan and his British sympathies. Although this was quashed at the eleventh hour by British and Gurkha troops from Singapore it was but a fore-runner for a campaign of aggrandizement against the old British Borneo now known as East Malaysia.

This huge area of tropical rain forest with its sparse population of Dayaks, Malays and Chinese seemed an easy and attractive target to Soekarno. Not only was its wide land border virtually indefensible but its sympathies to the concept of Malaysia were suspect.

'Konfrontasi' as Soekarno called it started off as he might have wished. Soft military and civilian targets were attacked with impunity by a mixture of Indonesian irregulars (TNKU) and regular Army (TNI). After a bitter colonial war against the Dutch the Indonesians knew their business and despite heavy reinforcement by British and Gurkha troops they tended to hold the initiative.

In mid-1964 the decision was taken to allow offensive operations against Indonesian military targets within Indonesia. They were to be known as 'Claret' operations and were to be politically deniable. In this way it was hoped to put the Indonesians on the defensive and wrest the initiative away from them. The architect of this strategy was General Walter Walker, a very experienced and able Gurkha officer who was fortuitously in command of the Borneo operations.

So it was along the whole length of the huge Indonesian border that British, Gurkha, Australian and New Zealand soldiers set off in a series of meticulously planned operations to snatch away the military initiative without which there could be no peace for the attractive, backward and vulnerable peoples of Borneo.

What follows is the story of one company of a Gurkha battalion employed on these operations.

OPERATION KINGDOM COME

Chapter 1

THE COLONEL'S PLAN

In his masterly history of the Second World War Sir
Winston Churchill described his feelings on being
summoned to supreme office by saying that he felt all his
previous life had been but a preparation for this moment. I
often felt the same about Colonel 'Nick' Neill. He
commanded a company of 2nd Gurkhas in the vicious
fighting against the Japanese in the Arakan campaign in
Burma and again throughout the long Malayan Emergency.
Fanatical Japanese and elusive Communist bandits had been
his trainers in the very specialised skill of jungle warfare and
he had remembered all their hard taught lessons. A man of
few words and those spoken with great consideration and
devastating directness he was an imposing leader of men, a
fine trainer and the ideal commander to launch 'Claret'
operations in the massive area of jungle, swamp, mountain
and river of which he was to become master. I saw much of
him since my company was battalion reserve and lived with
Battalion HQ in Lundu some ten miles behind the border. It
was in the old District Officer's house overlooking the river
and now our Battalion HQ that he briefed me for an
operation called 'KINGDOM COME'. Usually these
briefings included only myself and Norman Corbett the

Intelligence Officer, but today a certain Major Peter de la Billiere of the SAS attended upon our deliberations. Norman explained his air photograph mosaic which comprised wholly that area of Indonesian Kalimantan opposite us. He directed attention to the Indonesian river network on which most of their supplies were ferried and to the large Indonesian military base at a place of onomatopoeic satisfaction called Babang Baba on the main river. I noticed that it was only just inside the seven mile range of the 105 Pack Howitzer even when the gun was mounted on the most adjacent part of the border.

Colonel Nick in deep confidentiality then unfolded his plan which involved three 2nd Gurkha companies and one SAS squadron, in all about five hundred men. The force was to ambush simultaneously the Indonesian military supply network in a series of river ambushes spread over a ten mile frontage and operating five to seven miles inside Indonesia. My company was to ambush down river from Babang Baba at a point where the river curved towards the border and was just in range of the 105 Pack Howitzer when mounted on a border landing zone known as Kandai (See Map 3).

After the orders group I sat alone examining the air photos and weighing up the implications of the Colonel's plan. Since I was operating far from any other part of the force I had only to think of my own company. It was now the 7th of August and we were due to cross the border on the 14th so I had a week to prepare. My plan really had to fall into four parts. First the move of a hundred or so men, a 105 Howitzer and its ammunition and a radio rebroadcast station from Lundu ten miles to the border by helicopter. Next the approach march of my company through seven miles of swampy jungle. Third the setting up and executing of an

2

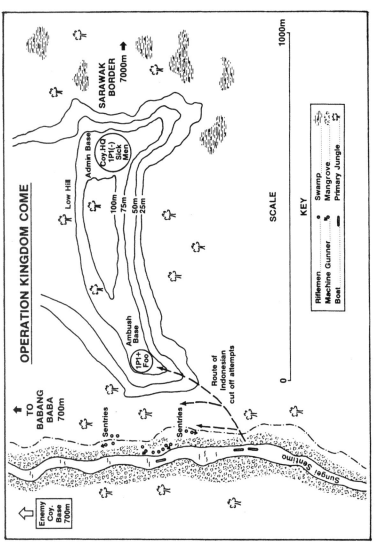

Map 4

3

ambush on the River Sentimo and last a return back to the border probably under fire and possibly under direct infantry attack. Having pondered for a while and made a few more notes I walked out into the main operations room where John Parkes the Adjutant presided ably over the nerve centre of battalion operations. With an ironic smile he handed me a box of air photographs covering the 'Claret' area and then returned to his evening situation report to Brigade. Leaving the photos to my long suffering clerk to sort out I went to where my company were playing volleyball cheerfully unaware of their future. After joining their game for a bit I settled down over a tin of Tiger beer with my second in command Captain Surendraman Gurung to discuss our future plans. Dark for a Gurkha, Surendraman although outwardly unimpressive was in fact a man of quite exceptional ability. Two weeks before whilst I was languishing in hospital in Singapore with some obscure virus he had commanded my company in a highly effective 'Claret' operation which had killed twelve Indonesians with no loss to the company. Together we had converted Support Company from three specialist weapon platoons to a closely knit and effective jungle going company which, whilst slightly smaller in numbers, could hold its own with the other rifle companies on any operation.

We had to use the six days left to us to the maximum benefit so that night after supper I sat at the table in my little attap hut and worked out a detailed programme. The next few days saw us busy from dawn to dusk in briefings, ambush practices, simulated withdrawals under attack, weapon firing and sharp shooting on our jungle range. Neither did we forget casualty evacuation using a helicopter

... In a seemingly limitless sea of swamp, tangled undergrowth and thorn ...

winch. At the end of some of these hectic days I remembered ruefully the advice to 'take it easy' on leaving hospital.

One of the main difficulties of this type of operation was getting to the right target area. There were no maps and walking through deep swamp for four or five days on purely a compass bearing was a real navigational test. This lack of maps was a grave disadvantage, and even when we did get them they left a lot to be desired, being dotted with great patches of sickly green annotated 'relief data incomplete'! Air photos we had but since the whole area was covered in vast primary jungle the usual ones from 10,000 feet gave very little information over and above the course of rivers. On the other hand the fact that we had to cross this great stretch of swamp and virgin jungle helped to achieve surprise since until a 'Claret' force attacked its objective it was very difficult for the Indonesians to know of its existence since there were few trails through the swamp and no habitation.

Administrative arrangements also needed a good deal of thought. We had to be able to go without re-supply for twelve days which meant that we could only carry those bare essentials to sustain ourselves, remembering that half our load would be weapons and ammunition. In the end we dispensed with the heavy army tinned rations and lived on a diet of sardines, dry biscuits, rice and a form of dried sprat known as 'Ikan Bilis'. This we bought from the local contractor in Lundu. We also carried one bottle of rum per man, a Gurkha custom determinedly retained and a large jar of Marmite per seven men to ward off the vitamin deficiency disease 'beri beri'. We were lucky in having been recently issued some light Australian sleeping equipment which consisted of a waterproof sheet, mosquito net and a light

Colonel D F Neill OBE MC
… All his previous life had been but a preparation for this moment.

Photo: N.T. Corbett

'Suspense' waiting for the helicopter

sleeping bag as well as a blow-up lilo. Despite paring everything the average man's load was eighty pounds with Signallers and Machine Gunners carrying well in excess of this. On the evening before we set off I explained to the whole company the general plan having briefed the Platoon Commanders in detail beforehand. I spoke in Nepali since the soldiers understood little English and anyhow, apart from John Masters my New Zealand Gunner Officer and his two signallers, all the rest were Gurkha.

This done I went over to the Mess and seated in an easy chair with a large whisky watched the tropical sunset and reflected how incongruous it was to be sitting in such comfort when in the next few days I would be soaked, covered in mud, bitten by leeches and insects and probably shot at by men I was yet to see. This aura of unreality was further heightened when after an excellent evening meal there was a showing of the film 'Campbell's Kingdom' set in the far North of Canada.

Chapter 2

REVERIE

In spite of a large nightcap I slept little that night. I always found it difficult to sleep before an operation started; tension and apprehension together conspired to rob me of the rest I badly needed. Fear also entered the equation, not really for myself but for Support Company lest my leadership fail them.

Such sleeplessness was not totally negative for in mental review of a forthcoming operation some hitherto unexamined facet occasionally came to light. That night it was a reminder to check the fuses of the 'type 36' high explosive grenades. We still retained a large number of these elderly but highly lethal hand grenades although the new American M26 grenades were slowly replacing them. The main drawback to the old 36 grenade was its fuse which had to be stored separately and inserted into the grenade just before an operation. In the humid climate of Sarawak the fuse tended to get damp and would then fail to work. If this happened in action lives could be lost so it was vital to check the fuse minutely for the tell tale pink discolouration before setting off.

This and other thoughts about the operation ran through my mind holding back the calming restorative of sleep. Outside a short but heavy downpour sluiced down onto the 'attap' hut roof whilst through the thin wooden partition the occupant of the next room steadily got into the rhythm of a soft, vaguely musical snore.

These factual and immediate thoughts gave way to generality and I found myself tracing back the various milestones that had led to me lying under the drapes of a camouflage mosquito net in a small dripping hut in what must be one of the least known countries in the world.

As with so many small boys, my first interest for things military started with toy soldiers at about the age of eight. Perhaps this interest might have waned or given way to others had it not been for another enthusiast at school called Colin Thubron. Our preparatory school, Heatherdown, rather frowned on the holding of large military model soldier collections on the premises so we agreed to meet in the holidays, our homes not being far distant. Thus started a long series of totally absorbing military manoeuvres. Both our armies consisted of superb Hamley's model soldiers and our battles were never constrained by time or geography. As a result Red Indian scouts could tangle with Bedouin horsemen and French Foreign Legionaries with Russian Red Guards whilst Cossacks and Life Guards might ride together in total amity! Colin's army was much larger than mine and was thus subject to large scale desertions to make mine up to strength. Strangely enough he never attempted to keep the finest and best painted to himself but relinquishing all else to his visitor would retain a series of chipped but battle hardened units for whom he had particular affection. Actually laying out our battle formations on his bedroom floor; writing up the history of our two opposing nations

(Bullockia and Thubronia) and drawing the necessary maps generally encompassed the first day. Calls to meals were reluctantly obeyed, those to go outside and get fresh air were honoured but only in the breach, whilst 'lights out' was stoutly resisted. The maid's attempts to tidy up were invariably repulsed. Thus grew a lasting friendship and although many years have passed since we deployed our armies the memory of those happy encounters remains fresh and bright.

Without doubt the two favourite units in my army were the King's Royal Rifle Corps (60th Rifles) and the Rifle Brigade known jointly as the Greenjackets. Their smart but subdued green uniforms, their rifles carried at the trail and let it be admitted their large bases which made them steady under fire all attracted me to them. I read their histories and bought Simkin prints depicting them; when my time for National Service came I determined to join them.

Some years later I found myself travelling down from Malvern College to London to meet up with my mother and step-father to attend a 60th regimental interview in Ecclestone Square. Although initially rather disappointed that my interviewing Major was not in full dress green uniform but a dark suit the rest was all that I had expected it to be. The walls of his fine office were hung with watercolours depicting riflemen in the Peninsula war whilst a silver bugle sat on his huge desk. The Major himself was handsome, dark and possessed a fine black head of hair and a military moustache; from all emanated the pleasant aroma of Thomas's 'Royal Yacht' hair lotion. Although I answered various mundane questions to the best of my ability I believe it was a combination of my very attractive mother and old Etonian step-father who swayed the interview in my favour.

That and a hitherto unsuspected relation whom it was found had Greenjacket connections. In the end I was offered a regular commission in the 60th Rifles provided I passed recruit training, got into Sandhurst and passed out successfully.

Whilst welcome this result placed me in something of a dilemma; I had actually only been seeking a two year National Service Commission it not having been my intention to make the services my career.

On the other hand I had no other ideas for the future and my rather modest collection of 'O' levels at Malvern were unlikely to commend me to any prospective employer.

Thus it was with considerable apprehension tempered by firm resolve that I walked through the gates of the Greenjackets Depot, Upper Barracks, Winchester. If the office in Ecclestone Square had conformed with my idea of the Greenjackets the recruit training platoon in which I now found myself definitely did not. We were fifty or so, mostly Londoners with a few dockers from Southampton and a sprinkling of public school, potential officers like myself. We occupied the top floor of a draughty barrack block which was reputed to have been built as a palace for Charles II. It was no palace now with bare boards, iron beds and two villainous coke burning stoves.

Our Platoon Commander whom we rarely saw was an effete and languid Rifle Brigade officer who appeared permanently fatigued. It was difficult to understand why because he never appeared to do anything. The real leader of the platoon was a small, dark cockney platoon Sergeant who went under the rather ominous nickname of 'Spider'. That he was talented militarily and a leader could not be disputed but that aside, his character did not bear close examination.

From the moment we arrived and he relieved us all of ten shillings towards platoon funds to the day he was finally rumbled, he and his cronies resorted to some very questionable ways of implementing their incomes. This was not difficult for his ploys were always subtle and not easy to pin down whilst most of his platoon were docile and fearful. By and large my ten weeks in basic training was endured rather than enjoyed; not because I found it difficult but because I resented the fact that such an unhappy and corrupt organisation could flourish as part of a unit for which I had such an immense regard. Nevertheless one adapts, and by the time I went up to take my Regular Commissions Board at Westbury we had the measure of Spider and he knew it. In vain he tried to threaten and bully us but for anybody who could survive a British public school in the fifties, recruit training presented few hurdles and slowly the platoon's innate sense of justice asserted itself, eventually exacting its just retribution.

'You won't pass,' pronounced Spider confidently as I set off in my thrice pressed battledress for the Regular Commissions Board at Westbury, but I knew I would; just as I had known I would win my weight in the House boxing finals at Malvern against all forecasts.

With the Regular Commissions Board successfully behind me I left the platoon to go to Beaconsfield where the Army School of Education were to attempt to bring my academic standards up to Sandhurst entry level.

As I slung my kitbag onto the top bunk of a warm and welcoming double room I reflected that matters had improved. They were to improve further with the arrival of my room mate, a charming, well read and amusing Light Infantryman. Freed of the harsh discipline and often mindless restrictions of recruit training we were able to enjoy the comparative latitude of a mainly academic environment. The evenings saw Nigel, my room mate, and I in the 'Old Hare' with a bottle of red wine in front of a blazing fire. There we patiently awaited the arrival of film starlets from the nearby studios. On the rare occasions that they did come they had no eyes for two private soldiers but that hardly detracted from our excitement at adoring them from afar. A comely middle aged widow was far more interested in us and would have probably given us valuable practical experience but with the perversity of youth we rejected her in our pursuit of the unattainable.

My two years at Sandhurst seemed in retrospect to have been a return to school. Probably for those who went direct from school it represented a new horizon but for us back door army entrants there was a certain feeling of 'deja vu'. My first term I found difficult because in addition to being driven from pillar to post again as in recruit training I had to pass a special army entrant exam at the end of the term. My maths had always been appalling so I had to work very hard; this meant weekends and holidays since there was little other free time. This was probably as well for as a result of a family crisis I had to live on my cadet pay which was very meagre. Strangely enough I quite enjoyed this period exploring the almost empty Academy on Sundays free from the military panoply of bawling Sergeant Majors and officious Cadet Officers. The library especially I came to love and visited it in the few free moments I had.

With the first term exams safely out of the way I began to lead a more civilized existence and made a few very good friends in the company of whom I had many enjoyable moments. Sandhurst taught me a lot of things but what it failed to teach me was my trade, the command of a platoon in battle; this could be considered to be rather a serious shortcoming although it did not worry me at the time.

During my last term at Sandhurst I had my final acceptance interview for the 60th with the Colonel Commandant. He was an eminent war time General but now terminally ill. The interview was little more than a ritual laying on of hands for I had carried out my part of the agreement and therefore the 60th would take me.

At the end of the last term we had the final batch of exams and although I knew I had done well at military history and enough in most of the others I was apprehensive at the maths result. It was thus with some trepidation that I heard that my Company Commander wished to see me. I need not have worried for all he wanted was for me to voluntarily relinquish the military history prize that I had apparently won in favour of an august youth who whilst having risen very high in the cadet hierarchy had failed to secure any prize which he could collect in the presence of his visiting father; also an august military personage.

I was very happy to do this although subsequently I rather regretted the three years free membership of the Royal United Service Institution which went with the prize. As for the cadet concerned he left the army shortly after commissioning so I doubt he availed himself of his good fortune!

Perhaps the greatest excitement of the last term at Sandhurst had been the trips to London with two other cadets destined for the 60th for fittings for uniforms. Outside Welsh and Jefferies in Duke Street the London smog swirled but inside old Mr Welsh personally supervised the fitting of our splendidly smart rifle green patrols with their discreet red trimmings and our black frogged mess kit jackets. It was with a tremendous thrill that I realised that the moment was fast approaching when I would join my Regiment. When a few weeks later I joined the 60th in Ballykinler in Northern Ireland I found my expectations not only fulfilled but surpassed. It was like joining an extremely select and well run club. Everything the Regiment did was done well and since the Riflemen were the Regiment's prime concern the standard of man management was almost awe inspiring. I joined with two other young Second Lieutenants one of whom was a close friend called Mike Eustace. We were promptly christened 'Bollock and Useless' and were received with kindness tinged with amusement. For our part we did our best to emulate our peers although this was difficult since nearly all of them were quietly outstanding as soldiers or sportsmen. The great strength of the 60th was their ability to absorb all manner of talents and allow them to blossom instead of attempting to cast all their officers into some alien mould as happened in some other Regiments.

Thus amongst this 'Jeunesse Dore' I learnt my trade. My platoon soon discovered I could not map read as did Mole my Company Commander. 'Hullo one Alpha this is one where are you?' Breathlessly 'One Alpha I am at Top Hat.' Mole (con brio) 'One you are not at Top Hat because I am at Top Hat and you are not here so where are you?' With mounting panic I realised I was attempting to set up a road block on the Southern Irish side of the border. A Guarda in green uniform approached, 'Now Sir would you be so kind as to take those fine boyos of yours back to the other side of the bridge because you are in Eire now.' That was 1960, the Irish border was a gentler, kinder place then.

I was teased gently; Mole sent me out every Saturday

morning in a Land Rover to map read; and I learnt this most necessary art which often escapes even distinguished army officers.

Nearly every Sunday Mole and Iona had me to lunch after church which we all attended in our Welsh and Jefferies 'Prince of Wales' check suits. At one such lunch Mole discovered I could not drive; next day lessons and a test were arranged with the Motor Transport Officer. It was a very caring organisation.

Perhaps equally as important as military experience was learning the art of living. In this urbane environment I enjoyed the lasting pleasures of classical music and literature, the delight of a winter's evening with the chessmen and a bottle of vintage port and the warmth of good and amusing friends. It used to be said of Greenjackets that the arrival of a visitor led to an exodus by the back window but I certainly never found this, although it is true that we were very happy with our own company.

At Christmas and in June we had balls. The Mess was decked out in flowers; a delicious cold table prepared by the son of a famous restaurateur presently doing his National Service in the Mess and a plane hired to bring girls and friends from London. None of this was done with ostentation but as part of the natural order of things. The girls when they arrived seemed gorgeous but for me almost totally unapproachable; conversation with them tended to reduce me to incoherency. Fortunately they were whisked off by the young Captains and Lieutenants allowing the likes of myself to enjoy the company of the equally attractive Regimental wives for whom there was no competition since they were already bespoke as it were.

At long last an opportunity occurred to distinguish myself

other than by leading my platoon into Eire. The battalion was to run an inter company boxing competition and it was vaguely felt that an officer should participate. 60th officers actually boxing seemed rather a contradiction in terms so it was with some general relief that I volunteered myself. I trained hard and after a couple of preliminary bouts knocked the battalion butcher out in the finals. When the Commanding Officer (who was God) presented me with my prize he broke the silence of several months to say 'Well done Christopher, I think knocking him out in the second round got just the right balance between skill and compassion.'

After various skill at arms and tactics courses I found myself back with the 60th in Berlin after a three month absence. The Regiment was the same but its environment much different. In place of the green hills of County Down was the huge city of Berlin slowly being reconstructed from the ashes and rubble of the last war. Still possessed of large areas of bomb damage it had an aspect of a strange twilight existence slightly resembling Graham Greene's Vienna of 'The Third Man'. Then it was possible to walk over to the Eastern part of the city relatively freely although the sense of pervading menace and totalitarian drabness made such a journey a depressing affair. We could also go to the two opera houses in East Berlin and I remember seeing 'Tosca' in a quite magnificent production, marred only by having to wear mess kit and thus fulfilling our predestined roles of swaggering Tsarists to which the Russian and East German propagandists could jab a finger 'to adorn a moral or point a tale . . .'. Perhaps I was too sensitive.

One hot Sunday in August whilst Duty Officer I received a call to get the battalion back into barracks in preparation for operational deployment; the East Germans were apparently building a barrier between the two halves of the city supported by the Russians. For three long hot days we waited in full battle order with live ammunition for the order to deploy. I believed then and still believe now that a vigorous response to the totally illegal action of the East Germans in dividing the city would have forced them to back down, but no orders came. So a flimsy barricade with countless gaps which we could have easily dismantled was turned into a major obstacle which soon became the infamous Wall.

After dithering whilst the East Germans completed their barrier we now became distinctly hawkish and deployed on the line of the barrier in the area of the Tiergarten. Shortly after we had taken up our positions an American armoured column on the way to 'Check Point Charlie' came to a halt on the edge of our administrative area, they had got lost and had arrived amongst the trellises of the rose garden. The situation was rapidly assuming the proportions of high farce. Nevertheless until Christmas we remained deployed and tried to look aggressively at the awful automatons on the other side in their Nazi type uniforms. During the occasional breaks we had from this tedious and by now very cold duty I managed to fall hopelessly in love with a very attractive Polish girl. We met in a student bar in down-town Berlin where I had gone to listen to a jazz band. Whilst wading my way through a vast jug of beer which came with the price of the entry ticket I espied a fair-haired rather ethereal girl with a group of students on the other side of the room. With amazing courage (for me!) I asked her to dance; she refused, I asked her to dance again; she again refused with rather less conviction but now her companions looked aggressive.

Gathering my last reserves of determination I asked yet again and she accepted, slight embarrassment touching her alabaster complexion with colour. Our affair was rather a difficult one since she had no proper identity papers and my profession called for extra special caution in consorting with anybody from the Eastern block. We met in romantic furtiveness in a dim little night club called 'The Blue Tattoo' in Bismarkstrasse. Christina was not only a very sweet girl but intelligent and cultured and in Poland had been reading for a medical degree. Her English was impeccable. Apparently her family was an old established one and thus not in favour with the Lublin government. Sensing the closing net she and her mother had escaped to freedom via East Germany to West Berlin.

Whether by chance or design I received notice of posting to the Greenjackets Depot as an instructor immediately after Christmas. Not only was I very sad to leave Christina but also the Regiment for which I had so much pride and affection. It was thus rather a morose officer who slowly sipped his after dinner kummel as the military train clattered through the uniform drabness of the North German plain bound for Antwerp and the ferry to England.

Remembering my own experiences of recruit training I was much relieved to find that the likes of Spider and his cronies had long been swept away, to be replaced by quite outstanding NCO's especially selected from the Greenjacket battalions. My fellow training Platoon Commanders were also a very talented and congenial crowd so all seemed well set for a pleasant two years. Recruit training however is by its very nature repetitive and soon a number of us were becoming restive to do something more interesting. Of the four training Platoon Commanders two went to the SAS for distinguished and gallant tours, I went to the Brigade of Gurkhas and one, possibly the wisest, went into his father's successful car dealing firm.

The idea of going into the Gurkha Brigade for a three year secondment was given to me by a close friend in the 60th who had decided upon such a course. The 60th and 2nd KEO Gurkha Rifles enjoyed a very close relationship since in the Indian Mutiny they had together held the Delhi Ridge against all the efforts of the mutineers to dislodge them thus resulting in the expulsion of the latter from the key city of India. As a result the two regiments enjoyed a close affinity even wearing similar uniforms and secondments were actively encouraged.

Thus after two congenial but fairly undemanding years I found myself pulling out of the snow and ice of London Airport for the exciting uncertainties of Hong Kong. On arrival at Kai Tak I was in a different world, a colourful noisy excitable world of slim chattering Chinese endlessly busy; of willowy beautiful girls in discreetly seductive Cheongsams whilst their Hakka sisters in black fringed hats worked with pick and shovel in the dusty streets. Fire crackers and shouting children surrounded our Land Rover as we cautiously picked our way through acres of densely packed squatter huts to the hills beyond which lay the New Territories. Suddenly the frenetic dusty streets ended and we were winding our way through shady trees and slowing down for troops of monkeys, whilst below us the huge reservoirs shimmered in the early morning sun. Then slowly descending to an immense bay we found ourselves in the unchanged rural China of the New Territories. Placid buffalo ploughed the rice fields and little villages nestled within their groves of bamboo whilst in the distance huge hills descended vertically to the azure sea on which floated picturesque fishing junks. It was all too much, and asking the driver to stop I paused to drink it all in.

The barracks called Queen's Hill was right in the north of the New Territories and consisted of about sixty or so acres of green huts, playing fields and training areas. A wonderfully smart sentry straight out of a Hamley's box saluted smartly, a calloused hand touching the edge of his diced board Kilmarnock hat, whilst at his side a highly polished kukri lay dormant in its sheath.

It being a Sunday there were few people about save the Adjutant, a quite charming officer who got me settled in and over a cup of coffee in a Mess redolent of the North West Frontier mapped out my assimilation into the fold. First a period in a rifle company as a sort of observer to learn customs and language followed by command of the mortar platoon for which I had done a qualifying course before leaving England.

Back in my room overlooking the hills and paddy fields I was able to turn over in my mind these new and exciting circumstances. My reverie was broken by the arrival of the young Gurkha detailed to be my orderly. He spoke a smattering of English which he shyly practised whilst unpacking my clothes; holding up my service dress he asked where I had put my medal ribbons. Embarrassed I had to admit to not owning any. To him this seemed almost inexplicable since Gurkhas were hardly ever out of action.

As I was soon to discover in a Gurkha battalion the best laid plans seldom reach fruition when it comes to officer career planning, and the forthcoming rash of formation exercises found me already in nominal command of the mortar platoon. I say nominal because whilst I attended battalion orders groups the actual running of the mortar platoon was carried on by an exceptionally able Gurkha officer called Surendraman, who will feature much in the subsequent pages. Knowing none of the language and having only recently passed my mortar qualifying course I remained in a state of perplexed surprise that despite frequent moves by mule at night the mortars always seemed to be in the correct place when wanted to support the battalion. Nevertheless I sensed that the Commanding Officer, a grizzled veteran of North Africa with one eye and a DSO was becoming increasingly suspicious of my bland assertions that the mortars were in position and ready to support him in whatever was to be his next manoeuvre. After one particularly difficult night march over what seemed to be every hill in Hong Kong, complicated by a sea crossing, he put matters to the test by demanding that I take him to the mortar line. With a sinking heart I wondered how on earth Surendraman would have managed to get his eight heavy mortars borne by mutinous and bad-tempered mules over mountain and sea to the eight figure grid reference we had agreed together in a pin prick of light in a howling gale. I personally thought it unlikely and saw my secondment being rather shorter than anticipated. As we got nearer the deep valley where they were supposed to be I got steadily more despondent and the Colonel increasingly suspicious. Then as the valley came into view I saw the ugly black snouts of eight mortars jutting from their superbly dug and camouflaged pits. Just then came a call for fire and suddenly the valley became a scene of feverish activity as ranges were adjusted and practice bombs slammed home. I was overwhelmed by relief and gratitude to Surendraman and there was perhaps a glimmer of amusement in his otherwise deadpan face which signified the start of our long and happy complicity. 'Lucky for you!' growled the CO as we climbed back up a small Matterhorn to reach Battalion Headquarters.

With the exercise season safely out of the way I then found myself in charge of the jewel in the Battalion's crown, its shooting team; due shortly to compete in Singapore with the pick of the Gurkha Brigade including that of the 1st Battalion. At first I contented myself with periodic appearances on the range to check that all was in hand. However after about a week of this the formidable Gurkha officer who really ran the team took me on one side and in poor but forceful English gave me a thorough dressing down.

Thereafter I lived, thought, ate and drank shooting. We were up with the dawn and in bed shortly after sunset. My Nepali improved and my admiration for my fellow marksmen and their dedication grew. We won the shooting just pipping a far from gruntled 1st Battalion and whilst waiting for a plane back I was able to explore with my sister battalion's young officers as guides the dubious fleshpots of Singapore.

However amidst all the fun and new experiences of being with a Gurkha battalion my intention was always to return to the 60th, to its calm urbanity, my friends and the biting cockney humour of its men. I would not have wavered in this had it not been for an unusual set of circumstances.

On arrival back from Singapore I was called to the Battalion Second in Command's office and sat in an armchair under the gently turning blades of the fan.

Lighting his Sherlock Holmes pipe he enquired if I was fit. This seemed a fairly innocuous start so I replied that I thought I was. He then jumped on me the quite amazing proposal that I form a team of twelve including myself and with another team from Headquarter Company represent the Battalion in the 'Round the Colony Race' in less than three weeks time. This gruelling race involved a number of teams running literally round Hong Kong, over hill, down dale, paddling across Tolo Harbour, with some cycling and an obstacle course thrown in for good measure; all in the burgeoning tropical heat of May. Every other Regiment especially the Gurkha ones had been practising for months and were supremely fit and ready.

Apparently the team that had been nominated to participate from 'A' Company had lost its team leader in a minor accident and as the rules stood could not thus run there being no substitution allowed. Since one British officer had to run and I was officially on the books of 'C' Company I and the unfortunate and unprepared 'C' Company were nominated. Without wishing to appear defeatist, I attempted to point out to the Second in Command the impossibility of us ever coming up to scratch in the time available. He was adamant, anyhow the Commanding Officer had much confidence in me he insisted. Such confidence appeared wildly misplaced at that moment; however one bright ray relieved the gloom of the situation; Captain Surendraman was now Second in Command of 'C' Company, perhaps he would have some ideas. When I got to the top of the small hill where 'C' Company's barrack block stood Surendraman was waiting for me with eleven of 'C' Company's best men. Some were ace basketball players, others gymnasts, others Khud racers whilst as my Second in Command a magnificently confident Sergeant called Gobinde had been nominated. After planning how we would conduct our training we split the team into its three component parts, one group of four running, another group of four running, and paddling a boat across Tolo Harbour and the other group in which I placed myself running, cycling and doing an obstacle course. Time was short and we met at four that afternoon for our first run which gave me time to cancel any private life I might have arranged for the next three weeks.

Thereafter we rose at three each morning, got on our trucks at four and having gone to some previously planned starting point would run from five until two when we used to meet up with the Headquarter Company team and our cold water and curry at a stream or beach where we would cool off. We ran in uniform olive green shirts and trousers and ammunition boots with a compass, map and two water bottles.

After our meal we would go off separately to teach the soldiers how to bicycle and paddle an assault boat and ended up with obstacle course training. It was a shattering regimen and I was asleep most nights by eight.

After a week of this I soon found out what superb men Surendraman had selected for me. They were all very fit and intelligent and despite our late start were soon shaping up well until a series of mishaps set us back. One morning our route took us along the lip of a reservoir high in the hills, unfortunately once on it there appeared to be no way off save by a sheer twenty foot drop down to the concrete catchment drain below. A strong young Lance Corporal called Bishnubahadur, a physical training instructor, managed to get down with a hair raising slither and jump and then helped the rest of us down. When it came to my turn just as he was supporting my foot on his shoulder I slipped dislodging a rock which crashed into his face snapping two teeth and cutting his mouth severely. One man in ten thousand would have continued helping me down oblivious of his own wound but Bishnubahadur was such a man. We were miles from anywhere so with blood pouring down his shirt he kept on running. That night the dentist removed broken bits of teeth and sewed up his mouth and next morning he was on parade again at four o'clock. I was much upset at the disfigurement I had caused this fine young man but with a pained and toothless grin he told me not to worry as he already had a wife!

Whilst we appeared to have caught up with other teams in most respects bicycling remained a weakness. Strange to relate in those days few Gurkhas could bicycle and I had to teach the other three in my team from the very first principles. By the end of the second week I had got them all successfully if rather unsteadily bicycling round the square but this might not be sufficient to enable them to tackle the steep slopes which they would have to negotiate in the competition. Under the rules we were allowed one practice on the competition obstacle course so I decided to combine this with bicycling down the competition course so as to recreate as exactly as possible the competition conditions. By pitching this three days before the competition proper I hoped that my three men would have reached reasonable proficiency.

In the event, after cycling most of the way with great confidence the front man inexplicably swerved causing us all to crash into him at some speed. All suffered quite severe grazes and bruises whilst one man lay in considerable pain on the road with his shoulder dislocated and twisted behind him. Bishnubahadur, himself further cut about, walked over to the man and putting his boot between his shoulder blades gave the arm a sharp jerk. With a sound we all heard the shoulder slotted back into place and the man staggered to his feet.

That night we held a council of war and decided to give up bicycling and run the distance carrying the bicycles. Although the man whose shoulder had been dislocated was still in pain and the rest of my team badly grazed we decided none should report sick lest we be barred from running. At this juncture Sergeant Gobinde pressed on us this theory of sucking tomatoes whilst running to stop stomach cramps from which we had all been suffering.

As I went back to my room to wash off the sweat and blood I slowly realised that these men were cast in a very unusual mould. Nothing was going to stop them winning; they were indestructible and indefatigable. Despite all our handicaps of time and training there had never been a moan or regret. I felt an immense, almost overwhelming affection and affinity for them and the grandeur of their simple courage and dignity.

On the day of the competition they ran like men possessed and the spectators that laughed at us running with out bicycles soon found that any time lost had been well compensated for by flawless navigation and a furious pace. On the obstacle course Bishnubahadur, seized by a frenzy of determination, literally threw the main with a damaged shoulder over every obstacle and at the end we would see that we were in the lead. indeed we would have won had it not been for poor Sergeant Gobinde collapsing. His team carried and dragged him for about five miles but the time loss just edged us out of victory. We put his collapse down to a surfeit of tomatoes and thereafter he was known as 'Golbera' which is Nepali for tomato.

This growing affinity was soon cemented by command of

a platoon on active operations in Borneo; there could be no going back. Thus it was that somewhat nervously I made my way to Penang where the 60th had moved prior to deploying to Borneo. The sight of my old friends made my mission that much more difficult but my mind was made up. The Commanding Officer was one Lieutenant Colonel Edwin Bramall MC, already an outstanding soldier and later to become a Field Marshal. With patience and understanding he heard me out and having pointed out the possible career disadvantages to what I was doing agreed to recommend to the Colonel Commandant of the 60th that my request for transfer to the 2nd KEO Gurkhas be granted. It had been a desperately difficult decision but, once made I knew it to be a correct one.

Chapter 3

14 – 23 AUGUST 1965

My orderly, a slim rather Caucasian looking Gurkha brought me some tea just after dawn and after dressing in olive green uniform and high lace-up canvas jungle boots I set off to the company to see how they were getting on. The day was overcast and cloudy and I wondered whether the big twin rotor Belvedere helicopter due to lift us would be delayed taking off from Kuching some thirty or so miles away.

The company had been up since well before dawn and were now doing a final check of their weapons and equipment. Weapons cleaned and lightly oiled, grenade safety pins firmly down, machine gun belts done up in khaki rags to avoid them glinting and so on. Most of the company had been carrying out similar checks before numerous operations over the past two years and they realised the importance of setting out with everything in order. Once across the border was no time to discover a broken firing pin on a rifle or forgotten detonators for grenades.

Very briefly I ran over the arrangements for the fly-in with Captain Surendraman and the Platoon Commanders. The Belvedere would arrive at eight and after refuelling would carry the artillery 105 Pack Howitzer, crew and ammunition to the gun position where they would be met by my Mortar Platoon Officer who had flown out the previous afternoon with four 81mm mortars and twenty men. The gun and mortars together would form a fire base designed to support my company in all phases of the operation and was commanded by a British Captain. Also at the fire base was the radio rebroadcast station for the operation which consisted of radio equipment and about twenty Signallers who operated their station from the top of a steep hill adjacent to the gun position. They had the vital task of maintaining communications between Colonel Nick in Battalion HQ and the 'Claret' companies. The base had to be able to protect itself against Indonesian attack so fire support arrangements also allowed for close-in defensive fire from the mortars should the base itself come under attack. It was a good base since as long as our soldiers remained firmly entrenched on top of the hill known as Kandai it was very difficult for the Indonesians to approach unseen.

After the gun had gone then my company would start flying out to Landing Zone Red 183 as it was named. Since all seemed to be under control I walked over to the Battalion operations room to see if there was any news of how the other companies were getting on. Norman Corbett, immaculate as ever, in cord slacks, chukka boots and a well pressed khaki shirt told me that 'C' Company were already across the border as were the SAS whilst 'A' Company was to move within the hour direct from Biawak, their base, which was close to the border. Norman then told me the rather disturbing news that Singapore had decided to leave the fledgling Malaysia. I was sure this must have weighty implications but my mind was too full of other things so I went off and got a civilised breakfast in the Mess. Eggs and bacon were unlikely to be much in evidence during the next week or so.

After a short delay, never surprising when operating with helicopters, a great Belvedere clunked over the horizon and deposited itself amidst the clucking hens in the village padang or square. The soldiers waited hopefully for its rotor downthrust to blow up the sarongs of the Malay girls watching on the grass. The girls realised this and when in a good mood allowed it to happen thus greatly contributing to the war effort.

The Belvedere having actually arrived was now thirsty and required copious quantities of fuel to animate it again. The pilot sweating heavily in his flying suit eyed both the rootling piglets beneath his machine and the assembled company with the same supercilious air.

Happily the smaller Whirlwind helicopter attached permanently to us was already started so I sent off Sergeant Chabilal and six men from the reconnaissance platoon to do a final check out on the landing zone in case the Indonesians had put pressure mines beneath the logs of the landing pad. It was his job to abseil down and pronounce the area safe. Sergeant Chabilal, a thick set phlegmatic Gurkha suffered from chronic back trouble and would not thank me for this task I suspected.

As we sat waiting for the message that the LZ was clear the company clerk came down with the morning's mail. A letter from my bank manager had stern words to say about my overdraft whilst my insurance company declined to insure my gold signet ring again. This was reasonable as I had claimed for two in six months both lost in the swamp.

Presaged by a small internal explosion the Belvedere's engines thundered into life effectively erasing a junior unmarried officer's few financial worries. By 10.30 we were all in to Red 183 and once everybody was sorted out we set off with the diminishing clatter of the last helicopter's rotor blades reminding us that we were now on our own. The weak sun had burnt the last of the mist away from the valley. Since the first part of our journey was in open scrub and low secondary jungle and thus unshaded, we all became damp with sweat which started at the back under the pack and soon enveloped the whole upper body. The recent heavy rains had made it very soft underfoot but after about half an hour we crossed the border and just before we got into thick primary jungle I caught sight of the gun position and was glad to see that the four mortars were already dug in with only their dull black snouts showing above the ground.

Once into primary jungle it became cooler because of the shade of the vast canopy of branches high overhead. This canopy of shade made it comparatively easy to walk through since the sun was cut out thus stunting the growth at ground level. Permanently in a soft twilight the effect was rather like walking into a cathedral. It soon started to rain cascading onto the jungle canopy thirty or forty feet above and only after about two or three minutes reaching us plodding far below. The rain quietened the continual whirr of cicadas and the screech of hornbills which were very common at that time.

Since this area was well known to us I had been tempted to follow some of our past tracks but in doing so we would have run the risk of being ambushed by the Indonesians. During our previous operational tour in 2nd Division of Borneo one of our companies had been badly ambushed using a track so

I had opted to go over the grain of the country on a compass bearing from the start; much harder work but safer.

That first day we were moving through an area that we had patrolled extensively before. It was quite hilly but dry and on average we were covering four hundred to five hundred yards an hour now which included a ten minute halt every hour which was vital if the soldiers were not to become exhausted. On these halts we all moved fifteen paces off our route and then taking off our packs rested while in each section the Machine Gunners remained alert. The soldiers could drink water and relieve themselves if necessary and chew biscuits if hungry but there was no talking, unnecessary movement or smoking.

I always found these halts useful to check our route and try and work out where exactly we were. With only the blurred air photo to go by I seldom succeeded.

We trudged on up and down hills until about four o'clock when I felt we were getting quite near the swamp and decided to make camp. This had to be a careful procedure since the company was at its most vulnerable when making camp, cooking and sleeping. Timing was vital, if camp was made too late it got dark and the soldiers' cooking fires gave away our position and if too early valuable daylight marching time was lost.

Having halted the company I sent out a patrol led by the leading Platoon Commander to find a suitable area for base. He came back after about half an hour having found a spot close to where the swamp began from where we could get brackish water. In heavy rain the company drew into a perimeter following a basic routine of clearing patrols, posting sentries and finally making base. The base formed the only element of rudimentary comfort in an otherwise extremely spartan environment. Gurkhas raised on the uncompromising soil of Nepal were quick and inside forty-five minutes the perimeter trenches were dug, the meal was cooked, water had been drawn from the swamp and the drum-tight shelters dimly glistened in the twilight. Whilst the soldiers were working Surendraman, the Platoon Commanders and the Artillery Officer gathered together and waited while I wrote down my orders for the next day. At this stage there wasn't much to say except that the next day we would enter the swamp and our progress would slow dramatically. I gave out the order of march and compass bearings and together we pored over the rather unhelpful air photo to try and find where we were which as expected we couldn't! The Platoon Commanders then gave me their reports, so and so had a fever, Rambahadur had slipped and twisted his ankle, Sergeant Chabilal's platoon radio was not receiving and so on. Within our limited resources I tried to ameliorate these difficulties but really we were on our own, there was nothing else available save that which we carried on our backs. The sick soldiers could be given aspirin or penicillin for their fevers and have their twisted ankles strapped and the radio set could be taken to bits, dried out, and put together again but above that there was nothing we could do. If a soldier was really ill we would have to carry him and if a radio set wouldn't work we would have to do without. Each night when base was made the gun and mortars were given a fire plan to cover us. Since it was not possible without a map to give our location exactly an approximate position had to be given with a safety margin and once the first shells or mortar bombs had burst then we would adjust the fire more exactly. This was all rather haphazard but it worked and the only time we got it wrong and a shell landed in the middle of our men it didn't go off. The Almighty through the medium of his swamp was very kind! By the end of another day we would be beyond the extreme range of the mortars so we would only be worrying about the gun which was a more accurate weapon.

During all this my orderly performed his daily miracle of domesticity. As if by magic, over our heads appeared a waterproof sheet, boiling tea was thrust into my hand and a dry towel chucked over my shoulders to stop me shivering. My simple bed was laid out, my rifle cleaned, my water bottles refilled, ammunition checked and foot powder and mosquito oil put near to hand. In no house, hotel or pleasure dome elsewhere have I received such devoted attention as I have from Gurkha orderlies. I often wondered how a simple hill farmer from the Himalayan foothills was able to show such care, forethought and sensitivity. Many visits to Nepal gave the answer; the Hindu religion which teaches regard for fellow man in a way that ours has never done.

As I sipped tea I wrote out a short message for Battalion HQ and my Signaller, a tough little character nicknamed `Jhamti' by his fellows sent it back via the radio relay station to a no doubt expectant Colonel Nick. An approximate grid reference using gridding on the air photo followed by NTR – nothing to report. Jhamti then whispered conspiratorially for a while on the set and came back with a message from Battalion HQ which told me that all other elements of the force were across the border by varying distances. It was in this way that I could roughly gauge how near they were to their target areas. Our infrequent and brief radio communications conducted in a

Captain (QGO) Surendraman Gurung
... longing for that close relationship of understanding and utter
support that I had enjoyed with Surendraman.

mixture of grid code and Nepali can't have given much joy to Indonesian intercept experts.

Surendraman then gave three long low whistles and quietly the soldiers pulled on their equipment, grasped their weapons and went to their 'stand to' positions. I often thought this was the most important event of the day. As I went round the perimeter with Surendraman I made a point of saying something to each soldier. Thus I could gauge their state of morale, health and tiredness. Each soldier knelt or stood in a trench with his weapon at the ready. I checked that they knew the password, the general tactical situation and the orders for the next day. Sometimes not all this information had percolated down to them but the very fact that I asked the questions ensured that their non commissioned officers kept them well informed. I was always particularly keen to ensure that the soldiers operating the switchboxes which detonated the protecting ring of 'Claymore' mines knew exactly where the mines were and similarly I checked the machine gun positions as it was they with their high cyclic rate of fire and the shock effect of the mines that would stop any enemy over-running us in a surprise attack for which dusk and dawn were the most favoured times.

By the time I had gone round the complete position it was fully dark and having stood the company down to eat and sleep guarded by our sentries I wended my way back to my shelter. Tiredness ebbed through me like a paralysis but my orderly somehow contrived to revive me. He guided me to my bed and having taken off my equipment I got out of my wet stinking clothes and into a dry shirt and trousers that he had all ready for me. He then gave me a mug with about two inches of neat rum in it and then faded into the gloom. As I sipped the rum I felt life begin to stir in me again and the tiredness and chill began to recede. All around me I could hear the muffled sounds of activity; eating, changing clothes and getting into the communal beds for three or four which the soldiers favoured for both warmth and convenience. All the time the rain dripped onto the poncho cape above my head. Rain was uncomfortable and dangerous. It soaked men and equipment, rusted weapons, clogged up radios and deadened sound so that an attacker could get close without being detected. After a while Surendraman came and as we sipped our rum we discussed how things had gone that day and how they were likely to go the next. Every evening we met thus and plotted the course of our operation and talked of all manner of things whilst our orderlies got our meal organised. Surendraman found the ban on smoking on the march very difficult to live with and as a result chain smoked until late into the night.

A little later our meal appeared from the gloom, warm rice, curried fish, lime chutney and curried potato – delicious! After two or three days the chutney and potato would vanish and before the end of the operation so would the fish; on the credit side our packs got progressively lighter. After our meal Surendraman went off to bed but the red glow of successive cigarettes showed him to be still awake.

At long last I slipped under my mosquito net and blanket hoping that no scorpion or snake had got there first. They were occasionally attracted to body warmth and the soldiers dreaded getting them in their communal beds. The scorpions could paralyse with their sting and many of the snakes were deadly – especially the red tailed krait.

As I lay there my thoughts always turned on how strange a circumstance it was that eighty heavily armed men should be sleeping in a hundred metre circumference circle in the middle of virgin jungle miles from home in one of the least known countries of the world. Occasionally a soldier would talk or moan in his sleep, a moan occasionally of pain or fear, occasionally pleasure dreaming no doubt of some soft-skinned hill girl in his arms only to wake to the reality of the damp dawn.

In the distance a tree crashed down and then another and another like dominoes, if they fell on us they would crush and kill sleeping soldiers – one just couldn't worry about such a possibility. I took a long swig of cold water from my bottle and slept.

A touch on my shoulder awoke me, putting out a hand I received a mug of hot tea from my orderly. It was 4.45 in the morning, dark and raining. An occasional glow from a hexamine cooker illuminated groups of Dante like figures packing up their beds, making tea and pulling on their wet clothes. A soldier bare to the waist stirred a pot, the light of the low flames playing on his shoulders and slim waist, he looked appallingly vulnerable in his nakedness. I shuddered at the thought of a high velocity bullet tearing into those finely etched muscles and bones.

Time to attend to the morning equation; the balance between a gulp of hot tea and the next wet garment, reeking of yesterday's sweat. Shake out the boots in case a scorpion was nestling in the bottom, lace them up and then help my orderly pack. Soon all the fires were extinguished and the company went to their trenches in silence, thus we remained until it was light enough to see well into the dripping jungle after which I stood down the company to fill in the trenches, finish packing up and get ready to move out. In this brief hour everything had to be done but experience made all the difference and my soldiers were invariably ready to move ten minutes early. So the long snake of heavily laden men made their way down into the swamp. The feeling of going up to the thighs in a slush of brown water and decaying vegetation was always abysmal.

So the morning drifted into afternoon plodding through the mire with only an occasional little dry island in a seemingly limitless sea of swamp, tangled undergrowth and thorn.

If the soldiers felt discomfort and fatigue they never showed it. On they plodded, weighed down by their massive packs but still alert and searching for sight or sound of movement. At one stage two little mouse deer ran along beside us unusually fearless. I suppose that apart from a few SAS patrols whose old bivouacs we occasionally stumbled on, few other humans ever walked these swamps which seemed not to have changed since time began.

Early in the afternoon we left the swamp and came across a huge area of fallen trees, twenty or thirty acres forming a massive obstacle to our progress. I climbed up onto the wreckage and could see the jungle rising up again beyond the fallen trees.

Giving everybody thirty minutes to rest and eat their hard tack biscuits and sardines I and Captain Surendraman wrestled with the problem of our best way to tackle this obstacle. There was no question of crossing it on our bearing as we would never get across by nightfall, at the same time it would be a long business working our way round it. In the end we decided to try and cross it at its narrowest point and changing our compass bearings accordingly started to clamber up the wreckage.

An exhausting few hours followed. Each man laden down

by his heavy load of kit, weapons and ammunition clambered up and down thirty foot piles of shattered trees and branches with the afternoon sun beating down mercilessly upon us. Occasionally we would be able to walk along some huge trunk for twenty yards or so or jump from broken branch to broken branch. The soldiers were incredibly sure footed but I loathed walking along these narrow trunks when one slip meant crashing down twenty feet to the earth below. There was no chance of stopping for a rest, there being nowhere to rest. Just before nightfall the leading platoon cleared the fallen trees and got into jungle.

By the time the whole company was in the perimeter it was dark and there was no question of carrying out our proper base routine. Having posted sentries I set the rest of the company to cooking the evening meal. This was the sort of time when people got ill, for unless closely supervised, soldiers in their tiredness would forget to sterilise the swamp water or take care of their feet and in the darkness it was difficult to ensure that all took their paludrine tablets. I heard Surendraman's gruff voice ticking off some non commissioned officer to ensure that despite tiredness necessary precautions were carried out.

The fallen trees had slowed us down considerably and taken us further north than I would have wished; the last thing I wanted was to arrive at the front door of Babang Baba! The next day I planned to keep walking all morning and then send out a patrol to try and find out how near we were to the river which was already assuming the proportions of a shifting mirage.

Next morning saw us back in the swamp and making slow progress but by late morning we got onto dry land and started walking along some low hill features. These seemed more promising as the air photograph showed a long crescent shaped hill on our side of Babang Baba.

Leaving the company on high ground I went with a small patrol to find out what lay ahead. Without packs and with only nine men we made good progress. After about two hours when I was wondering if we should find anything in the half hour that was left to us before we should turn back, the leading scout halted the patrol. I went to talk to him – he had smelt smoke. We sat quietly for a bit sniffing hugely and sure enough the distinctive smell of burning wood wafted in on my nostrils, faint but definite. Since the breeze was blowing from south to north it looked as if we must have come out to the north east of Babang Baba. The smoke was probably local Ibans burning down jungle prior to planting. I decided there was no point in going on since it was clear that in our efforts to get round the mass of fallen trees we had come too far north.

We plodded back and that evening sitting with Surendraman over our rum I could not help but feel rather disappointed at our lack of progress. Perhaps this depression sparked my fever for when eventually I got into my sleeping bag I felt hot and restless and disturbing thoughts turned over in my mind as I visualised some Indonesian patrol stumbling upon the tracks from our reconnaissance that afternoon. Such thoughts could, if allowed to germinate, turn a commander into the ultimate caution of doing the least possible commensurate with not being sacked. I thus reconstructed a fantasy conversation with my bank manager concerning the overdraft. He somewhat bedraggled in his wet and muddy sponge bag trousers having dragged his way through the swamp to confront me with my overdraft. Childish but enough to jerk me from the sense of prevailing gloom.

On the credit side the men were bearing up well and despite their exertions of the day before were now fully recovered having rested whilst the patrol was out.

The next morning we set off south west to try and get to the river below Babang Baba. After about half an hour walking downhill on firm ground we hit heavy swamp again and that first icy chill up to the thighs warned us that the next few hours would not be pleasant. The swamp was particularly bad and one soldier ahead of me disappeared up to his neck in mud and water having lost his foothold on a root. The man behind him pulled him out by his pack straps and on we went. The secret was to just keep jumping from root to root and wade slowly when there were no roots to balance on.

We went on like this until about midday when we started to climb out of the swamp onto a little island of firm ground. We had covered about two miles in six or so hours.

Having disposed of sardines and biscuits I left Surendraman to make camp whilst I set off with a small patrol led by Sergeant Chabilal of the Reconnaissance Platoon due west to see if we could find the elusive river.

For the first hour we were in swamp and twice I had to remonstrate with Sergeant Chabilal for going too far to the north of his bearing. Normally he was highly reliable but today he didn't seem very alert or receptive. At last we got out of the swamp into some low hills which seemed the same crescent of hills which ran to the east of Babang Baba.

We kept going until about 4.30 which was really the latest if we were going to get back to our base before dark. Nevertheless I was determined to get some hard information so forced Sergeant Chabilal to keep going against his protests. After about another fifteen minutes we came to a stream in the cleft of two small hills. As we walked down the line of the stream I became aware that at some stage the surrounding jungle had been cleared of undergrowth. Suddenly we heard voices and immediately hid in the sparse cover, seconds later a group of Ibans came down a path some twenty yards to our front. They were chattering amongst themselves and smoking cheroots. As they walked past I could sense their smell, an acrid mixture of cheroot smoke and rice wine. A small dog followed them and to my horror ran into the bushes where we were hiding; thankfully its owner brought it to heel with a gruff order before it discovered us but it was a bad moment! Our discovery by the Ibans would have compromised the whole operation as they would have immediately told the Indonesians.

After the Ibans had gone we heard shouting and chopping to our north so I sent an agile young soldier up a tree to see if he could see anything. He could – we were about a hundred yards South of Babang Baba which he could clearly see.

By the time we started back it was nearly dark and completely so by the time we got to the edge of the swamp. We radioed back to Surendraman to tell him exactly what was happening as the last thing I wanted was to be shot or mined by our own men.

The next three hours inching through the swamp in total darkness still remain clear in my memory. Eventually we literally crawled out of the swamp onto dry land but because of not keeping exactly to our bearing on the way out we could not locate our own base. Surendraman however was up to the occasion and by taking the risk of banging together two mess tins we were able to home in onto the sound. Thus eventually we got back exhausted but satisfied in that we knew exactly where we were in relation to Babang Baba. The elation of some positive information made light of my tiredness as did a steaming mug of hot tea. The rest of the company had spent a quiet day resting which was just as well as I was determined to reach the river next day.

Next morning I pushed the company hard as I was by this time despairing of ever reaching the wretched river. We had a number of sick soldiers with probably dengue fever which is caused by mosquito bites and induces a high fever. The contents of their packs were shared out amongst the others and they staggered along in a mournful little group at the back of the column under Surendraman's watchful eye. They should have been in bed in hospital but instead were confronted with several more days of jungle bashing. Before we set off I had chatted to them and encouraged them as best I could.

It was thus with considerable relief that at about 11.00 we moved up and out of the swamp and onto a low hill feature. Having had a short rest and eaten a tin of sardines and some hard tack biscuits I took a small patrol due west leaving the company to rest and John Masters our Gunner to work out whether his gun was still in range or not. The hill shelved steeply down to what appeared to be a disused path.

The sun burned brightly through the trees inducing a sort of park-like atmosphere to the bit of jungle we were walking through. Even filtered as it was through a tracery of leaves the warmth gave a feeling of well-being and hope. Leaving two of the patrol to watch the path the rest of us headed on into the thick bush. Soon we were in water again but this was different, it was clearer than swamp for one thing and colder for another and after a few more paces I realised that we had at last reached the River Sentimo. We pushed on a little further but soon the water was up to our chests and we were not even in sight of the river. Obviously the heavy rain had led to the Sentimo flooding all the surrounding area and it was going to be very difficult to reach the river proper. Nevertheless we had at long last found the Sentimo which was something so we returned back to the hill where the company was resting.

Over the inevitable sardines and biscuits I worked out a plan to send two patrols, one up river and one down river to try and find an ambush site. I decided to take the patrol going south and Lieutenant Nandaraj was to take the one going north whilst Captain Surendraman was to move the base five hundred yards or so further from the river and on the lee of the hill.

I then had a talk with John Masters about artillery support, he felt that his 105 Howitzer would just about have the range but apart from firing a ranging shell we couldn't be certain. What we did know however was that the gun could hit Babang Baba and it was from Babang Baba that we expected mortar fire once we had ambushed any Indonesians. I then got into contact with Lundu to tell them the good news that we had reached the river unseen. I could recognise John Parkes' voice on the other end, he seemed pleased. As far as I could gather from him the other elements of the force were finding it equally difficult to set up an ambush alongside the flooded river. I felt better having heard this as I had visions of all the other companies and the SAS comfortably in ambush whilst we had not even found an ambush position.

After a final few words with Captain Surendraman I set off with a small patrol from the Reconnaissance Platoon led by a very able young Lance Corporal called Birbahadur Pun. We soon came across the old path again further south but everywhere the water was just as deep, and after two hours searching for a way to reach the river I almost despaired. It was then that Birbahadur found an old logging track leading to the river where presumably at one time in the distant past the Ibans had logged the area and pushed the cut trees down a track to the river. The result was that by following the track the water was shallower and although up to our chests we could slowly make progress. One of our number called Minbahadur was a particularly short rifleman and the water came up to his shoulders. Inch by inch we edged our way along until at last there was the river, broad, muddy, flowing in brown turgidity from Babang Baba. It was nearly dark now but I took a few minutes to try and find somewhere to ambush. After a search Birbahadur and I came to the conclusion that all we could do was to make firing positions in the branches of the mangrove thickets and lie half in the water and half out. With this somewhat daunting thought we half-walked and half swam back to dry land during the course of which little Minbahadur slipped off the greasy logs under the water and nearly drowned, his jungle hat poignantly floating on the water below which he had disappeared weighed down with his rifle and equipment.

Thoughtful as ever, Surendraman had left a guide on the hill to take us to the new base which in the gathering darkness would have been difficult to find. We were cold and tired, and the dry clothes and hot tea that my orderly had ready seemed to be the most desirable things in the world at that particular moment.

After I had thawed out I got the Platoon Commanders together, and having found out from Nandaraj that he had been unable to get to the river I decided to use the very unsatisfactory area that I had seen that afternoon. Since the Anti Tank Platoon were all tall big men chosen for their strength to manoeuvre anti tank guns about I thought they would be best for wading in the deep water and so I told their commander, a certain Lieutenant Deoparsad, to choose ten really good men to ambush. I decided to take the heavy general purpose machine gun (GPMG) and a light machine gun (LMG) to give us the maximum volume of fire as our field of vision was limited and we would have to do the greatest damage in the shortest time. The rest of the Anti Tank Platoon I decided to leave on the path (see map at page 3) to ensure that no Indonesians cut us off before we got back through the water since it was likely that they would come down the path from Babang Baba as soon as they heard firing. The Reconnaissance Platoon were to go up on the hill overlooking the ambush and with them would be John Masters, since he would get the best radio communications from there to his gun which would shell Babang Baba as soon as the mortars there opened fire on us. Surendraman and Nandaraj and his Assault Pioneers I left in the base as a reserve in case the Indonesians cut us off and some form of diversionary attack was needed. The sick who now numbered eight, four of whom had high fevers, would also be in the base tended by the medical orderly. Trenches had already been dug in the base and I told Sergeant Chabilal to get his platoon to dig fire trenches on the hill next morning.

So after five days of plodding through swamp we were now

about to ambush. Suppressed excitement gripped me and drove away tiredness. Would they come or would the river be too fast flowing for any sane Indonesian to put a boat on? This and a thousand other possible complications flashed through my mind and despite my need for sleep kept me awake until the small hours. In the distance from whence we had come I heard the muted crash of a falling tree and I reflected on the dire consequences of a tree falling down on our base and its scores of sleeping soldiers. Soldiers so deadly with a weapon in their hands but so vulnerable gently sleeping under their frail `bashas'.

It was raining again, strange how depressing rain could be in the early jungle morning. The hopeful excitement of the evening before now gave way to slight foreboding at the thought of how amazingly vulnerable we were in our makeshift ambush position in the mangrove bushes. 'Chara jasto' -- just like birds – some rifleman had remarked!

When we got to the river it seemed if anything higher and the water colder. Taking great care not to get our weapons wet we slowly waded along the logging track with the water creeping up our chests with every step we took. We had left Lieutenant Deoparsad and the rest of the Anti Tank Platoon guarding the path. As we got nearer the time of ambushing Deoparsad got steadily more miserable and unenthusiastic. I now recalled his previous dubious reputation and determined to watch him closely.

Thus we slipped, stumbled and half swam to our ambush position. At the far right of the ambush I placed the GPMG, our heaviest weapon with its devastating high cyclic rate of fire. By laying branches between the mangrove bushes the two Gunners contrived a little platform to be on, half in and half out of the water. Then came a Rifleman and then myself and to my left Lalparsad the LMG Gunner and on his left another Rifleman. The LMG would spring the ambush on my orders and I had rigged him up a good fire position by using the hilt of my commando knife jabbed into the bole of a mangrove as a pivot.

As the hours ticked by we became very cold. The flood water seemed icy despite the hot tropical sun and for some reason the Gurkhas seemed to feel the cold more than I. So we waited with that swollen brown river rushing over our waists and legs all day until the sun turned to breathtaking gold and crimson and the daily spectacular of a tropical evening set in.

On the credit side we were in ambush, our plans laid and ready for anything that might come up river. Whatever the discomfort, this was preferable to staggering through swamp looking for an ambush position; Colonel Nick had ordered me to ambush the river and that's what I was doing.

Towards dusk two Iban locals paddled up the river in a dugout. We heard the flip of their paddles a couple of minutes before they came into sight and every man's forefinger was curled round his trigger in expectancy . . . an old man and a boy peacefully making their way up river. The man wearing an ancient trilby and shorts smoked a cheroot as he paddled, its smell wafting over the water. In front the boy sat upright, his hair coiffed in typical Iban style as with effortless rhythm he matched the strokes of the old man. Naked apart from a breech clout he was physically superb and the incongruity of his proximity to destruction was not lost on me. Although they both appeared to be looking directly at us I was fairly certain they had not seen us. The mangroves were thick and we were sited well back; they certainly gave no sign of having

Jungle base – The one hot meal of the day

seen or sensed us. I watched them round the bend of the river, the evening sun turning the river, boat and paddles gold in a scene of idyllic tranquillity. Finally all that remained was the smell of the old man's cheroot.

It was soon time to go. Forcing almost paralysed limbs to function, we slowly, painfully edged our way back to land and the relief of firm ground under our feet again.

Once back at camp there was a good deal to sort out since it was clear that the ambush could not remain in position all day and still be effective. It was during discussion with my officers that Lieutenant Deoparsad told us all of his conviction that we had been seen by the old man and the boy. He himself had not been in ambush but his men were and they had told him of their fears. I was sceptical and thought that Deoparsad was more probably suffering from cold feet. Fortunately communications back to base were particularly good that evening and having spoken direct to Colonel Nick I was glad to have his endorsement of my decision to ambush in the same spot. Nevertheless I did alter our route to and from the ambush position and arranged to change over the ambush party every two hours before they got too cold to be effective. However I determined that I would myself remain throughout since having marched so far I did not intend to miss action when and if it came.

Thus another day in ambush on the flooded river dawned and set. The only living creature to enter our ambush was a huge python which swam slowly upstream against the floodwater. I was very relieved that it did not decide to rest up amongst our mangroves – Minbahadur it could have managed quite adequately in one bite!

The next day dawned bright and clear as once again we

sloshed through the floodwater to our now familiar positions in the mangroves. The first ambush party were from the Reconnaissance Platoon and nothing happened during their spell. Next came Captain Surendraman and some Assault Pioneers. Surendraman had become bored with sitting in base all day and had decided to take his newly acquired Armalite rifle out for an airing. These changeovers were always rather fraught occasions as we were very vulnerable half wading and half swimming in the water and inevitably some noise was made. As a result I was relieved to have the Assault Pioneers firmly in position and the previous party out of the area.

At about midday we heard voices down river and all brought weapons to the ready. After what seemed a long interval a longboat appeared with four Indonesian soldiers in it, the one in the prow seemed to be wearing rank insignia. They all carried rifles except the third man who had a light machine gun across his knees and was not paddling. Our Machine Gunner with the GPMG opened fire at about fifteen feet range followed by the rest of us. The occupants were killed instantly and the boat overturned, a khaki cap drifted mournfully past me, separated for ever from its owner.

Moments later a flurry of shots spattered the river near to us and from the shots and crashing about in the mangrove down river it was clear that a substantial body of men were attempting to cut us off once disembarked from their boats. At the same time came the 'crump' of the first shell from our 105 gun landing on or near Babang Baba.

Clutching at mangroves to drag ourselves through the turgid water we struggled back to dry land meeting up with the Anti Tanks guarding our rear. Already we could hear the Indonesians shouting orders prior to attempting some form of attack. Speed was now of the essence and with water streaming off us we moved to the top of the hill where the rest of the company was waiting. After a quick check that everybody was present we moved off the hill back to our base in the swamp. I can remember intense irritation as John Masters our Artillery Officer slowly retrieved his drying socks and laced up his jungle boots. As we moved off he readjusted the 105mm to fire on the hill we had just vacated. A few minutes later the Indonesian attack went in on the now empty hilltop with what seemed at least a platoon. As they reached the top the first 105 shell landed nearby.

On arrival at our base in the swamp I was delighted to see that Lieutenant Nandaraj, who had taken over base duties for the day from Surendraman, had everything ready so that all we had to do was put on our packs and set off. I was relieved to see him as he only had twenty men or so and many of them had fevers or injuries. He was thus very vulnerable to any Indonesian cut off attempt. Also despite the strictest precautions we were always very aware of how easy it was for a nervous soldier to fire on his own men returning in the jungle gloom to base believing them to be attacking Indonesians.

After a few moments spent setting compasses and checking the air photos we were on our way south east in the hope that by taking a route that did not lead directly back to the border we would frustrate any cut off attempts by the Indonesians.

As we trudged through the swamp I had plenty of time to think about the ambush. Although it had been a limited success we would have done better to let the first boat go by and engage the second one which probably contained far more men. Nevertheless not being an entirely dedicated

'See no evil – Speak no evil – Hear no evil!'
Three young riflemen in thick jungle

A young soldier off on his first
'Claret' Operation

soldier I could not help but be secretly glad that only four Indonesian women would be without their sons, husbands or lovers as a result of our activities.

After about three hours and as night was beginning to fall we made camp on another island in the swamp. The company was tired but of very good morale after their success. That night I spent much time in ensuring that the trenches and other defences were laid out as well as possible bearing in mind the Indonesians were probably following up. It was well after nightfall that I finished visiting the sentries and by then we were all very tired. My orderly helped me off with my soaking clothes and after a few mouthfuls of rice I slumped under my mosquito net and slept, grateful to divine providence for our good luck.

M26 Grenade practice

Chapter 4

After two more days' marching we finally crossed the border and were picked up by helicopters. During our withdrawal the Indonesians had made no real attempt to harass us apart from firing their mortars off in rather a desultory way in our general direction. Since such efforts were only rewarded by much heavier artillery fire from our own fire base they soon gave up. By the time we crossed the border we had virtually finished our food and eight or nine soldiers had high fevers, but this apart the company only needed rest before they were capable of mounting another similar operation. I rather expected a two week gap before more 'Claret' as it were; so that the men could rest, re-train and re-zero their weapons.

This however was not to be, as I soon discovered after a very thorough debrief from Colonel Nick who seemed very pleased with our efforts. Apparently flushed by the success of KINGDOM COME (for it had partially achieved its aims), the Brigadier wanted to mount another operation in three days time. My heart sank as I knew I certainly needed more rest than that and I was fairly sure the company did as well. Anyhow the main point was that we were back in one piece and that night I intended to get rather drunk.

Thus it was and after several 'Rusty nails' (a lethal mixture of Whisky and Cointreau) after dinner in the mess I found myself drinking rum with the soldiers in one of the barrack room 'attaps' . Gurkhas have a great tradition of song and dance and into the small hours a succession of young soldiers stood up and sang and danced their tribal lays from the high Himalayan villages of Nepal. I was struck that although some of them could have been hardly more than sixteen their natural composure and dignity allowed them to sing without a trace of self consciousness. The paraffin lamp shone its soft light on strong brown upturned faces and high Mongolian cheekbones, the drummer tapped his 'madal' and the sad songs succeeded each other into the night.

Next morning I was summoned up to the 'Ops Room' to see Colonel Nick in his office. As I made my way through the swaying bamboos that protected and shaded the old badminton court I was conscious of primarily a severe hangover from the previous evening's totally delightful relaxations and secondly a feeling of marked apprehension at being required to carry out another 'Claret' operation before we had had a chance to sort ourselves out. For instance the soldiers with fevers needed time to recover; the weapons all needed re-zeroing and there were a number of new ideas I had developed that I wanted to try out with the company. Perhaps my most persuasive reason was the imminent arrival of twenty five new recruits from the Training Depot in Malaysia. Since I had several men due Nepal leave at the end of three years service I badly needed the recruits but without at least a week to train them up they would merely be a liability. Finally I needed a few days rest myself since so soon out of hospital the last week had left me feeling very drained.

In the operations room I found John Parkes who took me

'Claret' Soldiers with an admirer
'... Some couldn't have been more than sixteen'

quietly to one side and gave me a rocket for encouraging my soldiers to break the lights out order by drinking rum with them in their attaps until one in the morning! I vaguely remembered the Gurkha Duty Officer coming in and saying something rather official but since we all were far too intent on our songs and rum nobody took much notice of him. As John expressed his disapproval I saw the Iban and Malay laundry girls or 'dhobinis' as the soldiers called them coming across the grass to do the washing. They looked so colourful in their sarongs, green, yellow and red in the warm morning sun. Some were pretty too but disfigured by having front teeth missing. The subalterns in their prurient way ascribed this to a wish to facilitate some rather advanced sexual practice but it could just have been bad teeth! Some of the base soldiers such as signallers, drivers and clerks managed to enjoy the favours of these girls and pronounced them very affectionate. Unfortunately our continual absence on operations didn't allow my soldiers the same opportunities. For understandable reasons British officers in Gurkha battalions were expected to refrain from dabbling with the same women as their soldiers but rumour had it that one helicopter pilot was pleasuring a complete family of Iban dhobi girls. With these somewhat irreverent thoughts flitting through my mind I mumbled my apologies to John and waited for the Colonel to call me.

After a few minutes I was called in. The Colonel's office served as a sort of 'top secret' briefing room and one complete wall was covered with a large scale map of the battalion's operational area and on a separate section there were air photo montages of selected target areas. Sitting me down he talked over our last operation with evident satisfaction. The operation as a whole had been accounted a success and our part in it whilst small had been very effective. It had reminded the Indonesians that however appalling the weather conditions we could still strike at their river convoys and they were thus obliged to spare more and more troops to protecting their extended supply routes.

He had received confirmation from Special Branch sources on the other side of the border that four bodies had been brought in after our ambush, one of them a Regimental Sergeant Major – doubtless the fat one in the prow I thought.

I could feel he was very pleased by it all and in turn I was pleased for him since this jungle war represented the culmination of his many years service and for his battalion to be killing the Queen's enemies was everything to him.

At length he got up and beckoned me to the map and pointed out the village of Aachen in the centre of my operational area. Prior to our arrival in the Lundu area the Argyll and Sutherland Highlanders had carried out a very successful ambush just over the border on the main Aachen cross border track. Apparently since then the SAS had mounted small reconnaissance patrols along the upper stretches of the Sentimo some way to the west of Aachen village where it ran parallel to the border carrying supplies to the Indonesian army base of Berdjonkong. Recently Special Branch sources had warned that a large convoy of reinforcement troops and supplies would be moving up river to Berdjonkong in the next week. For this reason Colonel Nick wanted my company to be prepared to set off as soon as firm information was received about the sailing of the convoy from down river. To help me find the river in this area I was to be joined by an SAS Company Sergeant Major called Lawrence Smith who had been there before. I was not to be allowed to take any recruits and the Colonel accepted that the all up total of my company would not be more than seventy men. I would have a 105 pack howitzer and two sections of 81mm mortars to cover me from Kandai as last time.

After his briefing several questions ran through my mind but I didn't give them utterance. It was pointless wittering on about the men needing rest and administration when so much was at stake and speed was essential. The only really valid point was that I needed more men, because by the time we had left a base defence party and men had inevitably fallen sick with fever, I should only have about fifty men in ambush which wasn't enough to fight off a really determined Indonesian cut off attempt. However men from another company wouldn't know our jungle tactics and since there wasn't going to be time to teach them I didn't ask for them.

Colonel Nick then warned me to keep well clear of Aachen which had a company of Indonesians in it and some mortars and also to be careful when crossing the Aachen river which was to the west of Aachen and occasionally patrolled by the company in the village. This was a very tricky area and the stealthy approach to our target would be much more difficult than last time when we were walking through virgin jungle for much of the time. By the time we had finished it was nearly breakfast time. Back in Lundu we still clung to the traditional Indian Army breakfast served after a couple of hours at work at 9.00 and jolly good it was too with kippers, kedgeree, bacon and eggs and home made marmalade. Colonel Nick strongly believed in being comfortable and civilised when one could and that such comfort actually enhanced operational efficiency. So the Colonel, John

Parkes and myself strolled over to the Mess along the path flanked by hibiscus and bougainvillea planted no doubt by some conscientious District Commissioner many years ago. As we walked talking about our football team's chances in the Nepal Cup I was struck by the incongruity of this peaceful scene from which I was so soon to depart to the rigours and uncertainties of the Indonesian jungle.

At breakfast I met John Foley, an old friend of mine from the days of training Greenjacket recruits at Winchester. He had been leading an SAS patrol on the last operation and had heard the firing of our ambush from where he was. We had a long chat over breakfast and afterwards comparing notes about the operation. I was relieved to hear from John what an excellent man Company Sergeant Major Smith was reputed to be. As we sat chatting the Mess orderly came in with a note from Norman telling me to come up and see him in the Operations Room. This I did and he told me that our probable departure date was the 30th, it now being the 25th. This was good news as it gave me more time to carry out some preparation.

So it was − for the next two days we worked really hard re-zeroing everybody's weapons, practising casualty evacuation and most important of all accustoming the company to our new idea of a box ambush. Hitherto we had used the traditional line or linear ambush which although effective was very vulnerable to being outflanked at its extremities. Obviously much depended on the type of ground on which one was ambushing but given a reasonably flat area one could by forming the ambush into a box shape more easily fight off a counter attack from left or right. It was, like so many good ideas, Surendraman's brainchild and in the event it was to save the company from destruction.

First of all we practised it 'by numbers' on the padang football pitch and this had the advantage of the soldiers being able to see the complete layout of the ambush which of course they couldn't in the jungle. Probably as important as the ambush itself was the technique of withdrawing platoons back to a central strongpoint with pre-dug trenches from where, aided by artillery fire, they could better hold off the probable Indonesian counter attacks. We repeatedly practised this in great detail so that every soldier knew exactly where his place in the ambush would be and how he would make his way back to the strongpoint. Withdrawing under enemy attack is always difficult and we had to ensure that the Indonesians were never in a position to cut us off from the strongpoint or the company base. This could only be achieved by withdrawing those parts of the company not under direct attack to the strongpoint, and then withdrawing troops directly engaged with the enemy so that as they followed up the retreating Gurkhas they were suddenly confronted by a heavy weight of fire from the strongpoint. Artillery had a major part to play since it would fire on the perimeter of the strongpoint and serve to break up the Indonesian attacks.

During this time our recruits arrived after a very long journey up river from Kuching in an open and rickety boat. Despite the effects of their journey they looked a good lot and although I couldn't use them across the border I got permission for them to guard the fire base at Kandai since it was now becoming rather an obvious target for an Indonesian attack.

With training going well, the sick recovering and our plans developing and with many hours gazing at air photos behind me I was summoned to the Operations Room on the morning

Returned patrol awaiting pick-up on a border LZ
Photo: N.T. Corbett

of the 27th August to meet the Brigadier who had just flown in with Sergeant Major Smith in a helicopter.

Brigadier Bill Cheyne was a tall strong man, slightly balding with an engaging and direct way of talking. He was a Highlander and until taking over command of West Brigade in Borneo had never served with Gurkhas before. Shaking me warmly by the hand he congratulated me on our last operation and then told me that the convoy had sailed up river from its main riverine port of Siluas and thus we were to set out tomorrow.

My heart sank as I saw my carefully gauged programme of preparation dissolve into a frantic rush to get organised in time. After the exchange of a few more civilities I took Sergeant Major Smith off to his hut and then went on to warn Surendraman and the company of this change of plan. Throughout the rest of the day and much of the night the company got ready. Rations were packed up, weapons checked over, ammunition stowed and the gun and mortars made ready for flying out.

At six that evening I gave my briefing in the office to the 'orders' group. Captain Surendraman darkly calm; Sergeant Chabilal of the Reconnaissance Platoon loyal and dependable if not very bright and Lieutenant Deoparsad of the Anti Tanks fleshy and shifty and not greatly trusted after 'Kingdom Come'. Next came Corporal Bhagtasing commanding the Assault Pioneers instead of Lieutenant Nandaraj who had gone for three months leave to Nepal. Nandaraj was actually due six months leave after three years but was only getting a shorter time since he was needed back. I was very sorry to see him go as he was a fine officer but he had not been well and after fourteen months on operations was very tired. Bhagtasing was very junior but he was competent and determined. Then came Captain John Masters our New Zealand Gunner who had always done us so well. Tall, older and more senior than I, he was the elder statesman of our organisation and destined to play a vital role in the forthcoming operation. Finally came Sergeant Major Smith of the Special Air Service; an unknown quantity but already inspiring confidence in his firm and positive demeanour and general aura of easy professionalism.

My plan was fairly straightforward. We would set off from Kandai and head north west to take us well north of Aachan after which we would turn south west until we hit the Sentimo which flowed through the garrison village of Berdjonkong. Sergeant Major Smith would tell us when we had reached the target area after which we would lay our ambush. Simple enough in design but like all plans subject to unpredictable factors such as enemy, weather, terrain and luck or lack of it.

After giving my orders I strolled over to the company attaps and talked to the soldiers. They all seemed to be cheerful and confident and as so often before and since I gained strength from their robust and determined attitude. Their packs were ready and weapons checked and scrupulously clean. The attaps smelt of a mixture of rifle oil and curry powder.

It was nearly dark by the time I got back to my room where a young soldier was waiting outside the door. He introduced himself as Rifleman Bhimbahadur Pun one of the new recruits and said that Captain Surendraman had detailed him for the operation since my usual orderly Prithibahadur was still down with fever. Colonel Nick had said that none of the recruits should go over the border but he was obviously desperately keen to go so I decided to keep quiet and take him; we needed every soldier we could get. I explained how I wanted my kit packed and where I liked to carry things on my webbing. His intelligent eyes showed he understood all I had said and I felt that as ever Surendraman had made a good decision. This young man who was then probably about sixteen was to prove himself a quite exceptional soldier in the next few days but of this I had no inkling as he brought me a large whisky from the Mess which I drank sitting on the veranda of the attap immersed in thought.

The prospect of action like news of a mortal disease was a great stimulant to putting affairs in order and surveying the achievements and disappointments of life. My mood called for more whisky and Edith Piaf. Bhimbahadur dealt with the whisky whilst I put the record on. Subjected to what to him must have seemed discordant wailing Bhimbahadur dismissed himself leaving Edith Piaf 'Regretting nothing' under the tropical sky.

Perhaps the sad music made my thoughts turn to mortality. So far we had been extremely lucky in terms of casualties; none in the company so far this tour and very few last tour in the second division of Borneo. Other companies had suffered far more heavily; naturally one wondered whether our luck would hold.

So another departure day dawned. Bhimbahadur rallied around with tea whilst I surveyed the various weapons and accoutrements that comprised my inventory for 'Claret' operations.

First the self loading rifle of undoubted effectiveness. Although it was heavy I felt safer with it, knowing what it could do. Next the pack, vast and ponderous, like Pilgrim's burden and containing food, clothing, ammunition, bivouac and much else besides. Next the waist webbing equipment slung with water bottles, knife and ammunition pouches. Like Shaw's old soldier in 'Arms and the Man' I carried grub in one pouch as did everybody else – sardines, biscuits and chocolate. Finally a pair of green jungle boots beckoned me looking like shot rhubarb.

Certainly my most useful piece of equipment was a waterproof wrist compass with a luminous strobe. My mother had kindly got it for me from some rather smart shop in London. It was very accurate and its needle was quick to settle so by looking at it like a watch I could continually keep a check on the bearing. As a result we seldom strayed – I have it still today, battered but functional.

As I was lathering soap over my face preparatory to my

Setting off on a 'Claret' operation

last shave for the next ten days or so the morning procession of village 'dhobi' girls came into the camp to do the laundry. One of them was particularly striking, tall, beautifully proportioned with a jade green sarong tightly fitting over the swell of her thighs. I grinned at her and she smiled back that easy lazy Malay smile showing unusually a perfect set of teeth. I reflected rather ruefully on the unnatural existence we were obliged to live.

Before going to check out in the Operations Room and have breakfast I went over to the medical centre where some of my soldiers were still languishing with dengue fever from our last operation. They were disappointed not to be coming with us and touching in their wishes for good fortune. Their greatest desire was to get a bravery medal so one operation missed was to them a lost opportunity.

As I was chatting to them Howard Manual our doctor came in. Beckoning me over he gave me a mild rocket for helping myself to penicillin tablets without his permission – I generally found I could bully the Gurkha Medical Orderly into dispensing them on the quiet and they seemed to stay my recurring fever which had flared up. As he reminded me the trouble was that I had not done what the hospital had told me and taken a month's leave in the cool of the Cameron Highlands in Malaya to recuperate. Instead I had come straight back to go out on our last operation. With an eloquent shrug of his shoulders he gave me some huge and vicious looking green and black tablets and intimated that he knew better than I what was the best medicine. Howard was a kindly and companionable man with a charming wife and they were both definite assets to battalion social life. Although English Howard affected a certain Transatlantic style with cigars and a propensity for loosing off firearms. Little suspected by either of us at the time he too was to be plunged into the swamp the realities of which soon eclipsed the make believe glamour of the saloon shoot out.

As I made my way to the Operations Room the rain that had been falling intermittently all night now started to sluice down so that I was soaked on arrival. Norman Corbett the Intelligence Officer was ready with the latest news of the helicopter lift. 'Gun and mortars at 8.30 and the company at 10.00' he shouted as he ran to a telephone.

I went back to the company, checked all was ready and then went to the mess for breakfast, the last civilised meal I was likely to get for some time. Lieutenant Julian Parish, our Signals Officer was also having breakfast before taking the shuttle plane back to Singapore prior to returning to England to do a light helicopter pilot's course. Julian was my closest friend in the Regiment and the only person with whom I could really unburden myself. Together we shared the same interests, warmed to the same friends and enjoyed a similar brand of humour and approach. The thought that he would be away for the next few months depressed me. Together we talked of what we would do when we got back together again. Our plans were always grandiose but seldom came to anything. Julian bolting the last of his toast and marmalade dashed, late as ever, for the revving Land Rover which was to take him to the airstrip where we could already hear the old 'twin pin' Pioneer about to land. Not unnaturally perhaps I wondered whether we would meet up again. The fates were kind to me however but not so to him, for shortly after being best man at my wedding (for which he was nearly late again) he was killed in a civilian air crash, leaving a void that could not be filled. Just as I was about to go and get my kit on I bumped into Colonel Nick on the Mess steps, he was wearing his specially tailored waterproof cape known irreverently by Julian as his 'Garibaldi'. He had come from talking to the doctor and wanted to know how I felt. As always he spoke with great thoughtfulness and sincerity. I assured him of my fitness less he forbade me to go – even at this late hour. He looked at me straight in the eyes as if to bore through them and extract the truth; after what seemed an interminable pause he turned on his heel with a smile and went into the Mess.

Bhimbahadur had already taken my pack to the helicopter landing zone so strapping on my webbing and rifle in hand I went off to where the Mortar Platoon and Gunners were waiting to be picked up. Captain David Thomas, a couple of years older than I was to command the fire base which included as usual about twenty signallers perched up on top of Bukit Kandai running the radio rebroadcast station. David, I, the Mortar Officer and the Artillery Gun Position Officer talked finally over our plans as the ungainly Belvedere helicopter came into view and like some great broody hen cautiously lowered itself onto the padang. As the 105 gun was fastened underneath it on straps the Whirlwind helicopter set off with David and his advance party of signallers. Another company had cleared Kandai LZ so we were spared that chore. Once the Belvedere had lifted off another Whirlwind came in from Kuching and before long Sergeant Chabilal and the Reconnaissance Platoon were heading the company fly out.

I was rather touched to see that our company clerk, Corporal Kishanbahadur had come down to see us off. Traditionally clerks were not operational soldiers and anyhow they were needed to keep abreast of the paperwork whilst we were away on operations. Remembering his gesture and the rather wistful way in which he had looked at us leaving I later wrote a few lines of what Julian described as truly ghastly rubbish!

Base Wallahs

We never heard the sound of battle nor felt its fright
But we worked manfully to keep the files all right
Sometimes we saw them trooping back from war
Saw their tiredness and their wounds so sore
Base Wallahs! They laugh with a weary shake of head
But only we can laugh when they are dead

As usual I moved off with my orderly and radio operator

after the first platoon and whether as a result of Howard's pills or the coolness of flying high in the helicopter, my fever began to ebb. I was immensely thankful as at its worst it slowed me down physically and mentally so that my plans became influenced by personal considerations.

On arrival at Kandai there was a mass of activity, the mortars and guns being dug in, the new recruits digging slit trenches and putting up wire around the perimeter and signallers toiling up Bukit Kandai with batteries and heavy rebroadcast equipment. In its fickle way the sun had come out and its warmth sent little clouds of steam off the wet soldiers.

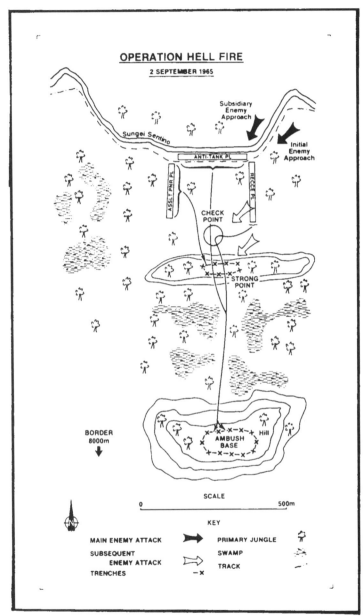

Map 5

Chapter 5

28 AUGUST – 3 SEPTEMBER 1965

Before long we were in and with Sergeant Major Smith with the leading platoon we set off at about midday. By the time we were off the gun position it was already raining again dripping in heavy drops through the trees and making the gloom of the jungle more forbidding.

After about half an hour we came upon what looked like a recent resting place for about forty or fifty men. There had been some cutting. I was initially concerned lest an Indonesian company had been in the area with the intention of ambushing us. On reflection however I was inclined to think it was probably 'A' Company who had cleared Kandai for us. Either way there wasn't a great deal we could do about it so we pressed on across the grain of some quite hilly primary jungle.

At about 2.00 we halted in an open area of jungle and spreading out in our normal defensive layout prepared to rest in the warming sun which was now slanting through the unusually well spaced trees. I was just looking at my own 'home drawn' map and trying to equate it with an air photo when I heard a gasp of pain from Surendraman who had joined me from the rear of the column. Running over to him I found him liberally splashing mosquito repellent oil over his bared arms; he had been bitten by a little column of mites that had run down a tree upon which he was leaning. Old soldier that he was he immediately recognised them as scrub typhus mites. Although we moved off immediately six soldiers and John Masters had been bitten which meant in all probability that after four or five days they would be delirious with fever. I considered sending those bitten back as we were still close to the border but a small group of heavily laden soldiers was particularly vulnerable to ambush and anyhow there was just a chance that if we dosed them with penicillin they might not be affected.

Towards about 5.00 in the afternoon we found a hill suitable for a base and made camp. We had only covered about a thousand yards owing to the various delays. As usual the well practised routine of searching the surrounding jungle, digging trenches, getting in water etc went on with quiet efficiency. I went over to where the two medical orderlies, one Gurkha, one British, were dishing out pills to the soldiers bitten by mites. The British one was an RAMC medical Corporal from Liverpool who had volunteered to accompany us. He looked far more miserable than the soldiers he was treating and I tried to cheer him up. In the event my sympathy was misplaced since on return to his Headquarters in Kuching he accused the company of drinking untreated swamp water on the march and as a result I got a tremendous rocket from the head doctor, a Lieutenant Colonel, in Kuching. I stoutly repudiated the story knowing that the medical orderly had mistaken drinking with soldiers splashing swamp water over their faces to cool themselves. However the medical Lieutenant Colonel regarded support company as a suitable corporate case for unstinted medical guidance. On his next visit to Lundu he arrived with a sandbag full of little marker flags for us to put round the area of jungle in which the soldiers had been bitten by scrub typhus mites to warn other units. The idea was so ludicrous that I nearly laughed which would have further put me into his black books. It was not until I told John Parkes the story that the realisation dawned on me that he probably had no idea we were operating inside Indonesia, so closely guarded was the security of 'Claret' operations.

Like so many figures of fun this same Lieutenant Colonel was to become the main agent in a succession of misunderstandings that were to affect Colonel Nick's subsequent career. However I always remember his first visit to us shortly after we had arrived in Lundu. He came and gave us a long lecture on field hygiene and showed lots of charts as to how to construct the best type of 20-seater lavatory in the forward company bases. He was obviously very suspicious of Gurkhas and the reason for this came out whilst he was drinking a gin before lunch in the Mess. Apparently at his urging the Scots Guards in another operational area had built a superb 20-seater that was the pride of his heart and which he showed to every visiting medical dignitary. Since it was in reality just seats over a gigantic cess pit it tended to get full of various unpleasant bugs which were best disposed of by throwing a white phosphorous smoke grenade down the pit once a week. Eventually the time came for the Scots Guards to go and with great pride they handed over this edifice to an incoming Gurkha battalion. During the handover something was lost in the translation because the next that was seen of this glorious loo was a massive explosion throwing hessian screens, wooden seats and excrement in all directions. Apparently the young Gurkha company medical orderly

A Reconnaissance Platoon machine gunner
(Lance Corporal Ramparsad Pun MM) who opened the
fire fight on Operation Hell Fire

hadn't quite hoisted in the white phosphorous bit and thinking that the pit could do with an initial take-over clean had thrown in a high explosive grenade!

Sergeant Major Smith's shelter was close to mine and whilst jotting down a few notes for my evening orders I noticed with admiration his self sufficiency. Politely refusing any offers of help he had put up his 'bivouac' in record time and was now extracting from his voluminous pack a special radio set. Having slung the aerial he proceeded to tap back his report to SAS HQ in Kuching in code. After he had finished we got into conversation and I was struck by what a sterling character he was. We were basically agreed as to our position on the air photo and it was clear that by heading north west all the next day we should, given our current rate of progress, cross the Aachen River well north of the dangerous village after which we could head for the river through what looked like being swamp most of the way.

My recruit orderly was now proving his worth and as soon as I had got back from inspecting the trenches at stand-to he handed me my dry clothes, had ready a mug of hot sweet tea, gave me his rifle whilst he cleaned mine and then went off to gather together the orders group into the little nook he had made them protected by a poncho cape and with little leaf seats to keep their bottoms dry. Given his youth and inexperience I thought this was exceptional. I was right -- he soon sailed up the Gurkha ladder of promotion never putting a foot wrong.

My orders for the next day's march were fairly perfunctory as we huddled in the renewed rain poring over a damp air photo by the aid of a pinprick of light from a shaded torch. After they had gone Surendraman and I drank our rum and ate a plate of 'bhat' made tasty by dried shrimps and lime chutney which was retailed by the local contractor in Brylcream jars collected from the soldiers who greatly favoured this hair dressing. It seemed an eminently sensible use of resources! Surendraman didn't seem to be any the worse for his mite bites but it was early days. We chatted in a desultory way for a few minutes with only the faint glow of his cupped cigarette in the black immensity of the jungle. With great regret I realised this would be the last time I could count on his wisdom, courage and resource for he was due to return to Nepal on six months leave as soon as this operation ended. He was probably the most battle experienced of all the Queen's Gurkha officers having been involved in a number of actions as a Platoon Commander in 'C' Company during the battalion's last tour in Second Division. Nearly all his operations were 'Claret', conducted in a dangerous open area of scrub and secondary jungle. During some of that time I had been Intelligence Officer and I knew better than most what risks he ran by operating in an area where there was so little cover. His Company Commander, the gallant Jon Aslett, at the time put him in for a Military Cross but he never got it. However I managed to get him mentioned in despatches for the operation he commanded whilst I was in hospital.

Tired I was glad to get into my 'bivi' which Bhimbahadur had prepared so neatly for me. Then I lay for a while savouring the dark immensity of the jungle above me. It gave me a feeling of incarceration in some massive vault that pressed in on our frail encampment from every side. On return to base after an operation I often used to sit of an evening on my hut's little veranda and gaze at the milky way. Just looking so high seemed to bring back a basic freedom denied me whilst in the jungle.

That night my thoughts turned to England with a nostalgia that was almost painful. The first signs of autumn would be apparent now; misty mornings with cobwebs hanging thickly on gradually fading foliage, warm days scented by tobacco plants. Above a great red harvest moon would be shining through the dust raised by combines working through the night to bring the harvest home. I wanted to survive this, and see the immutable change of the seasons and smell again wild garlic in the autumn lanes.

The dull smudges of cooking fires woke me. It was nearly 5.00 and looking over to Surendraman's 'bivi' I could see the glow of his cigarette. Soon daylight would come and he would not be able to light up again until darkness fell so he was building up his nicotine bank against the forthcoming period of deprivation! Hardly able to credit my good fortune I realised that my fever had gone; I still felt weak but otherwise normal. A few moments more and Bhimbahadur materialised in the gloom bearing a mug of hot sweet tea; firmly gripping my hand he clamped it on the tin mug handle – a sensible precaution as a boiling mug of tea spilt all over one's precious dry sleeping gear would be a minor disaster.

That day we made good progress and despite the steep hills we arrived at the Aachen River by early afternoon. Putting out strong flank guards on left and right I told Corporal Bhagtasing and his Pioneers to bridge the river which whilst not very wide was deep and fast flowing. The jungle in this area was quite thick with no traces of human movement or habitation so I felt that we had probably gauged our crossing place correctly and providing a boat didn't come down the river whilst we were crossing the Indonesians would remain ignorant of our passage. As the

Pioneers worked away I got back to Battalion HQ on the radio but they had no further information or instructions. During the morning's march John Masters our New Zealand Gunner had twice missed the line of march and had gone wandering off into the 'ulu'. Since his artillery group consisting of four men followed directly behind me I had only become aware that he had strayed when the leading scouts of the next platoon had signalled me to halt the column whilst they looked for John. In this thick jungle it was very easy to lose the man in front especially whilst negotiating an obstacle. If this happened I found the answer was to look low and listen. By looking low where there were gaps in the foliage I could often catch sight of the feet of the column. If this failed by listening one could often hear the creak of equipment or when in swamp the sucking sound of jungle boots coming out of the slime. I had been doing this for about three years but until I became experienced in the jungle it was quite unnerving to find the front man disappeared from view, leaving me leading the remainder of the column to I knew not where. What I failed to realise was that even now John was feverish with scrub typhus which makes his subsequent actions even more remarkable.

Eventually I got the signal from the Pioneers that their bridge was ready and went to inspect it. They had felled a strong tree over the river at its narrowest point and then had put a firm handrail made of vines alongside. It was a good bridge and we crossed and dismantled it without any incident.

By late afternoon we had climbed to the top of a steep hill and made base in a naturally strong hilltop position.

That night it bucketed down with rain and I thanked our good fortune that we were on a hill top and not a low island in the swamp. As rain dripped steadily onto my legs having penetrated my waterproof sheet I began to think again of homely things. What would my mother be doing now in her tiny and immaculate flat on the Sussex coast so many thousands of miles away? Were any of the millions of normal families heading off for their annual holidays thinking of us in the middle of the Indonesian jungle? In England the swinging sixties were then in full rhythm without me being able to enjoy this liberalisation from post war austerity. Thus I lay feeling vaguely aggrieved as through the hiss and gurgle of the rain a tree crashed dully to the ground in the valley below. Suddenly in the darkness there was a shriek of pain and then the frenzied movement of several bodies – 'biche-biche' I heard a soldier mutter. Some poor unfortunate had been bitten by a scorpion driven by the rain to find shelter in a four man 'bivi'. Sadly this was a fairly usual occurrence resulting in the soldier being in agony and unable to carry his pack for about twelve hours after. We gave him a shot of morphine and awaited the dawn.

Next day we set off in heavy rain and were all soon soaked. After marching for about two hours we hit deep and very treacherous swamp. I waded up to the front of the column which was moving very slowly and met up with Sergeant Major Smith to discuss where we were. He very frankly admitted that his previous patrol in this area had been in drier weather and there was much less swamp. Now the whole area was covered in three to four foot of water and he had no idea where he was. As a result I decided to find an island in the swamp, establish a temporary base and then unencumbered by packs send out a reconnaissance patrol to try and find out how near we were to the river.

After about another hour of plodding through the swamp

we came to what appeared to be a gently rising shelf of dry land culminating in a distant ridgeline. Leaving Surendraman to make camp I set out to reconnoitre with Lieutenant Deoparsad, Sergeant Major Smith and a patrol of twelve men from the Anti Tank Platoon. Since our bearing led us back into the swamp we were obliged to plunge again into a virtual quagmire through which we made very slow and exhausting progress. Even Sergeant Major Smith after all his time with the Special Air Service admitted to having seldom tried to patrol through more difficult terrain. The worst aspect of the area was that in the swamp there were flowing streams some of which were six or seven feet deep and unless one was extremely careful it was easy to mistake the stream for another piece of swamp with uncomfortable results. All the time the rain continued and the darkness and dankness of this swampy jungle stretching on for what seemed eternity was immensely depressing. How I longed for the warmth of the sun on my shoulders and some dry hill jungle with the light shining through it!

We paddled about in the swamp looking for a better way through and then finally returned to base just before nightfall tired and frustrated having achieved apparently very little. However negative information is better than nothing and it was quite obvious that endeavouring to move seventy men or so through the swamp we had just encountered made no sense whatever if any better way could be found.

Surendraman had made base well up on the ridge line and said that his base clearing patrols had found that the ridge continued as far as they could determine in roughly the same direction. I felt that tomorrow's best plan would be to follow the ridge for so long as it kept roughly west hoping that it would drop down to the river.

We discussed this at our evening council of war and we were all agreed that following the ridge line was the wisest course. We had been marching for three days now and were still no wiser as to how near we were to our target area. Already two of the men bitten by the scrub typhus mites were feeling ill plus the usual crop of twisted ankles and backs caused by slips and falls. As I sipped my rum that night I was far from easy as to our present situation. The company on this type of operation was like a pendulum which had to hit the enemy whilst swinging forward; if not the effect of appalling terrain, monsoon weather, illness and lack of proper food led to a falling off in their alertness and confidence. In this sort of warfare alertness was vital for it was the ability to hear or see the enemy first that literally made the difference between life and death. Confidence too was desperately important since once it ebbed belief in the ultimate success of the operation started to wane.

Unusually it dawned fine and with a feeling of almost exhilaration I watched the first shafts of gentle sunlight pierce through the trees and touch upon the damp shoulders of the soldiers as they packed their bivouacs up prior to setting off for the day's march.

I had carefully briefed my lead Platoon Commander who was Corporal Bhagtasing and also Sergeant Major Smith who played the role of 'eminence grise' to the operation that they were to follow the ridgeline for as long as it roughly conformed to our westerly bearing. I had no means of telling how far it ran but even if it only continued for five hundred yards or so it would be better than trying to get through the equivalent distance of swamp.

Having packed up camp, drunk a mug of tea, and eaten a

packet of 'dog' biscuits we set off up the hill heartened by the firm going and the sun high above the trees.

Soon after starting the lead platoon did a small detour from its line of march and soon after came the whispered message 'sap'. 'Yes' – there amongst a few dry leaves curled a little red krait, deadliest of the jungle snakes. Only the length of a man's hand, its venom could only be countered by an immediate injection of serum of which, of course, we had none. Thus seventy or so men trod circumspectly round one small snake which twitched its little head from side to side conscious of danger but unable to locate it.

Looking up the line of march and above the heavily laden bowed and patient men the sun cascaded through the trees brightening the colours and setting a troop of monkeys chattering in pleasure at the warmth on their bodies. After about ten minutes the halt sign came down followed by the signal for me to go forward. Accompanied by my orderly and Signaller I walked along the column occasionally exchanging a smile with a soldier on the way. Gurkhas take quite a long time to get to know but once one has succeeded in gaining their trust they remain the closest and most loyal of comrades. Since they give their comradeship sparingly many of their critics label them as lacking in rapport and disinterested which could not be further from the truth. To become accepted by Gurkhas is difficult but once accepted a Gurkha is the most devoted and indefatigable of comrades.

After walking up hill for a bit we suddenly dropped down a steep escarpment and after hitting a patch of swamp and making our way through some low trees and thicket we came upon the river not two hundred yards from the base of the hill.

Signalling the column to halt and putting out a machine

gun detachment to each flank I crept stealthily towards the river with Corporal Bhagtasing and Sergeant Major Smith. The ground in front of the river was a flat slightly raised alluvial plain covered in thick stunted trees and bushes and dropping quite steeply down to what looked a small and shallow river. Sergeant Major Smith confirmed that this was indeed the right river.

As we crawled forward to the river just short of it we came upon a newly cut path. Both the local Ibans and Indonesian soldiers used to cut the undergrowth away with parangs and by looking at the wood cuts we could see that this path had been recently cleared. In the soft mud we could also see the clear imprints of Indonesian army boots amongst the bare footmarks of Ibans or local porters. As we examined the path a boat containing three Ibans slowly made its way up river circumventing fallen trees in the river and sandbanks with difficulty. In spite of recent heavy rain the river seemed low and difficult to navigate. We lay pressed to the ground whilst the boat slowly made its way out of sight. It occurred to me that the river was too low and obstructed to be navigable by supply boats and for this reason the boats probably stopped well down river and supplies were then portered up under escort to Berdjonkong along the newly cut path by the side of the river.

What seemed very strange was that on the last ambush the river downstream near Babang Baba had seemed huge and yet not far upstream here it was really quite small. In subsequent discussions with Surendraman and Sergeant Major Smith we came to the conclusion that last time the river had been in flood whereas this time in spite of recent heavy rain the river was quite low. Another solution was that there were a number of branches of the river upstream but there was little evidence of this from the air photos which showed the river to be quite large even at Berdjonkong.

Clearly we needed to have a good look round to site an ambush so keeping the Platoon Commanders and a protection party of Pioneers I sent Surendraman back with the company to make base at the top of the small hill we had spent the previous night upon. It was a good strong position with a stream flowing through the swamp at its foot.

The ambush presented a dilemma because although we had been tasked to ambush the river the evidence of our eyes suggested that a supply convoy of big boats would be unable to navigate the river and its cargo would have to be portered along the newly cut path up to Berdjonkong. An ambush sited to cover the path wouldn't be able to see the river whilst an ambush covering the river could easily be turned by an enemy of any strength coming along the path.

After a good deal of thought and discussion and having had a look at the whole area, I decided to place the ambush on the path but to put a look out either side overlooking the river so that if the Indonesians did manage to come by boat the lookouts could warn us and we could crawl towards the river in time to ambush them. Unfortunately this plan had two main weaknesses which I did not foresee. The first was that it presupposed that the lookouts would hear the hum of motors or splash of paddles well before the boats got near and secondly it did not take account of how difficult it was to move a heavily armed ambush forward covertly and quickly.

Having decided on a plan I then allotted the platoons their areas. The Anti Tanks under Lieutenant Deoparsad were to be the killing area platoon and the Pioneers and Recce were to be left and right flank protection platoons respectively. In the rear of the ambush I decided to leave the check point party consisting of my Radio Operator, John Masters, the Artillery Officer and his two operators, the Gurkha Medical Orderly and the Company Sergeant Major. I positioned myself in the middle of the Anti Tank Platoon who were to spring the ambush. Some might well question why I did not stay with my Artillery Officer but to me the vital thing was springing the ambush properly and supervising a clean withdrawal. John Master's job would be to silence the enemy mortars in Berdjonkong once the ambush had been sprung and before they could start ranging in on it. There was thus little requirement to adjust artillery fire until we had returned to our firm base back on the hill. Behind the check point before the swamp started again I had noticed a slightly raised piece of ground protected on both sides by two massive fallen trees. Here I placed the strongpoint or RV which the ambush party would withdraw to before making their way back to the ambush base. Slit trenches would be dug on the RV so that we could fight off any attempt by the Indonesians to outflank us. This would give us a useful protected strongpoint at which to pause whilst withdrawing from the ambush should things be not going to plan.

The 'modus operandi' was for the Anti Tank Platoon to spring the ambush and then the Pioneers or Recce would fight off the likely counter attack, dependent from which way it came. Whichever of the latter were not committed would go back to man the strongpoint having been checked through by the Sergeant Major at the ambush check point to ensure nobody was missing. After they had safely occupied the strongpoint the Anti Tanks would withdraw using the same procedure and finally whichever platoon was in contact. This method ensured the maximum protection during withdrawal and good control which was vital if this tricky operation was not to end in confusion.

I spent about two hours planning the ambush and on return was glad to find that Captain Surendraman had got the company hard at work digging a really strong position. After a cup of tea, biscuits and a tin of sardines I gathered the 'O' group together and went through the plan in great detail using a model I had made on the ground. By last light I hoped our base would be ready with deep slit trenches dug for every man whilst a fatigue party from all platoons was sent off to dig and camouflage trenches on the strongpoint.

That evening I went round and talked to every man, told them of the plan and their part in it. As ever they responded wonderfully, even t ose with bad fevers. As I chatted to Surendraman over a rum that night I felt confident that plans were as well laid as thought and experience could make them.

During our previous nine month tour in Second Division I had been a Platoon Commander. My Company Commander was a very experienced soldier called Major Johnny Lawes. I could not have hoped for a more patient or wiser officer to begin active service with. He impressed upon me the importance of ensuring that every plan was exhaustively thought out and that the soldiers knew exactly what was expected of them. Additionally he never failed to give me the chance to operate independently and learn by my own errors. With such experience I found it second nature to examine any plan for snags over and over again. This plan was no exception but I should have known that in love and war things seldom go to plan.

As the early sun filtered through the tracery of leaves we moved into ambush. The Sentimo was obscured by the steep bank but we could hear it gently gurgling as it pushed its way round some obstruction.

Looking over my shoulder I had every reason to be satisfied; either side of me silent impassive figures sat relaxed but alert with their rifles laid ready to hand in forked sticks. On my immediate right sat the GPMG Gunner with his gun resting on a log that we had dragged forward. His belt of ammunition lay curled under a covering of twigs and leaves like some sinuous and deadly serpent. It would be my signal to him that would spring the ambush but since GPMGs had an irritating tendency to jam on the first round I was ready to fire the first shot myself with my rifle. The Anti Tank Platoon covered a footage of about twenty five yards that included two GPMGs, three LMG's and eight riflemen. To either flank were the Recce and Assault Pioneer Platoons out of sight to me because of the low foliage but checked in position. In addition to their normal weapons each platoon had three of the highly effective Claymore mines two of which they placed backed against trees facing up the track to either side of the ambush whilst the other they placed to the rear in case the Indonesians should try and outflank us.

This was really the first moment that I felt easy since I had been tasked for the operation. Here we were in ambush as ordered thus whatever the future might bring we had carried out our part and upon some distant map in Whitehall a little blue circle on an obscure Kalimantan river would be marked. In my naivety I imagined Generals in the Ministry watching our progress with nervous anticipation. With the benefit of hindsight they were far more likely to have been wondering how quickly they could pull out of South East Asia once this troublesome business with Indonesia was over!

Behind the ambush the check point was in position and John Masters sat shoulder to shoulder with his signaller ready to call his gun to fire on Berdjonkong. Behind them protected by two huge fallen trees was the RV with its trenches.

The day wore on, a sharp downpour soaked us but the sun dried us again, little steam clouds rising from each man. Rifleman Jumparsad Gurung the young GPMG Gunner next to me impassively chewed his quid of 'kaini' tobacco and lime, extra especially alert, conscious of his close proximity to 'Block Sahib' his Company Commander. The sun was overhead now it being midday and feeling the pangs of hunger I carefully pulled out a packet of 'dog biscuits' and chewed feeling their gluey matter work into that part of my stomach that was given to rumbling when hungry which was much of the time.

A troop of monkeys swung high in the trees across the river oblivious of our silent vigil and further down the line a man broke wind, drawing a furious stare from Lieutenant Deoparsad who was on my left -- then the boats came.

Two long boats each carrying twelve fully armed Indonesians glided upstream noiselessly propelled by two Ibans in each boat using long poles. By the time the lookouts had jerked the vines to warn us the boats were in the ambush area. The thought of losing such an ideal target overruled my caution and I signalled the Anti Tanks to crawl forward. Long seated in the same position and mentally adjusted to ambushing the path they were slow to react and by the time we were in sight of the river the second boat was disappearing upstream. I was just in time to catch sight of the rear soldier in the second boat who was European;

Russian, Dutch, who knows? Had they seen us? This and a thousand other thoughts rushed through my head.

It struck me that there might be more boats in the convoy; after all Colonel Nick had said it was a big one. Quickly I moved the Anti Tanks onto the river and re-adjusted the rest of the ambush. Although we waited until dark no more boats came and, conscious of a sense of failure, I ordered the company back to base.

Once back I called together the 'O' Group to try and piece together what had gone wrong, and more important, where we went from here. As if in sympathy with the prevailing mood the rain started to patter down. Bhimbahadur my orderly however was not to be put down by the gloomy atmosphere and rallied about with tea, dry clothes and finally a slug of rum from a mysterious source for each member of the 'O' Group huddled together under the waterproof poncho cape. Lieutenant Deoparsad sat bolshy and apprehensive convinced as he had been on the last operation that we had been seen and not best pleased by my criticism of his men's slow reaction. Sergeant Chabilal and Corporal Bhaktasing still rather unsure of what had gone wrong and Captain Surendraman deep in thought. The two Europeans John Masters and Sergeant Major Smith waited patiently for the steady murmur of Gurkhali to cease and for me to start talking English to them.

Punt poles were really the simple cause of our failure to destroy two boatloads of Indonesians. The lookouts had expected to catch the sound of engines or paddles well before the boats got into sight. As it was the punt poles made very little sound and so they got no prior warning until the boats were opposite them. Nevertheless I reckoned that after four hours or so in ambush the men had lost the edge of their alertness. The other point was that I had miscalculated just how long it would take to get fifteen or so heavily armed men, stiff from sitting in ambush, to the river side.

There was however no point in crying over spilt milk and basically there were three courses open. First to assume that we had been seen and beat a hasty retreat to the border. Second to continue to ambush the path and thirdly to ambush the river. Lieutenant Deoparsad was all for going home; Sergeant Chabilal and Corporal Bhagtasing hadn't really any strong views and so I, Surendraman, Sergeant Major Smith and John Masters were left to talk it through. Surendraman had been in charge of the base and Sergeant Major Smith had been there also with a hacking cough that precluded him from being in the ambush so they had not seen the boats. Nor for that matter had John Masters since he had been back with the check point.

The point at issue was that if we continued to ambush and the Indonesians knew of our presence then they could simply come round the back of us cutting us off from our withdrawal route and then attempt to destroy us. How successful they would be in this was doubtful but it was not an attractive thought so far inside Indonesia. On the other hand it was easy to take council of our fears on these occasions and remembering our ultimate success in a similar situation last time I determined to ambush the river and hope for the best. Having once made the decision the way was clear to try to ensure that in so far as possible if things did go wrong we were well prepared.

To this end I gave a very thorough briefing on exactly how we would withdraw if we came under attack and realising the vital importance of our dug in base if things went awry I decided to leave another five men and an additional machine gun with Surendraman. Surendraman himself was as ever a tower of strength and absolutely supported me. He admitted later over what must have been his tenth cigarette in a row that things could turn very nasty if the Indonesians had seen us!

Eventually I curled up in my blanket and whilst the rain spattered from the dark canopy of the forest wondered if at this very moment the Indonesians in Berdjonkong were finalising their plans for our demise.

It dawned clear and by the time it grew light enough to distinguish colour we were ready to move.

As the soldiers went through their final checks I got the 'O' Group together again to run through the plan for the last time. Five days on half rations, the nervous tension and the sheer effort of moving such a weight of weapons and equipment through the swamp showed in the tired, used look on their faces. The two Europeans were unshaven as I was myself, since the water was far too disease ridden to risk leptospirosis unnecessarily by shaving. This made us look much more dishevelled than the Gurkhas whose smooth skins only needed the occasional hair plucked out with a little pair of tweezers that they habitually hung round their necks on a string with their identity discs. However even on their normally impassive faces the hollows of tiredness around their eyes gave the lie to their even features. Looking at my own face in the mirror I had found myself almost unrecognisable, a dirty stubble tending towards a goatee beard, deep rather feverish eyes and a wasted hollow cheeked look that reminded me of those poor unfortunates I had seen lying under newspapers below the arches of the Embankment.

Sergeant Major Smith much to his disappointment was

still coughing badly and so had to remain in base which in the event turned out to be very fortunate.

By the time we got to the ambush area the sun was shafting gently through the trees and the cicadas were already bringing the night's calm to an end with their feverish whining.

I can remember distinctly the sun streaming through the trees and the GPMG Gunner flicking a large wood ant out of his GPMG breech mechanism when automatic fire, steadily increasing in volume, broke out from the area of the Reconnaissance Platoon on the right. My first reaction was that the boats had come the opposite way to that expected and that Sergeant Chabilal had opened fire prematurely. This annoyed me as had he let the boats come into the centre of the ambush we could have made short work of them. Whichever way more firepower would be useful and shouting at the GPMG Gunner to follow me I ran towards the sound of the firing. By the time I reached Sergeant Chabilal a furious fire fight was in progress; foolishly I was still standing but soon got down after a burst of fire seared through a sapling near to me. Through the noise of short staccato bursts punctuated by the splatter of small arms fire and the crash of grenades and Claymores he told me that the Indonesians had come down the path and were now trying to work their way round the back of the ambush. Chabilal said he could keep them at bay for a bit but the further they got round his flank the more difficult it would be for him to delay them. Infuriatingly the GPMG Gunner hadn't come as ordered, a GPMG would have greatly enhanced the Reconnaissance Platoon's firepower.

Telling Chabilal to hold firm I dashed back to the centre of the ambush. As I arrived the Anti Tank Platoon started firing;

aghast I thought they were firing at the Reconnaissance Platoon in error but with relief found they were engaging an enemy rocket launcher team firing at them from the other side of the river. Firing now seemed to be coming from all round as I got the two Platoon Commanders from the Anti Tanks and the Pioneers together and told them the situation and outlined my hasty plan. Bhagtasing and his Pioneers I told to go and hold the strongpoint as quickly as possible, once he was in position I would pull the Reconnaissance Platoon back through him and then back to the ambush base and after them the Anti Tank Platoon. Fortunately we had frequently rehearsed just this eventuality. I told Bhagtasing to pick up the checkpoint party on his way. Quickly the Assault Pioneers moved back whilst amidst a hail of fire I ran back to Chabilal. As I did a salvo of mortar bombs straddled our position – where was our artillery?

On reaching Chabilal I found the Reconnaissance Platoon dangerously exposed with Indonesians all round them, miraculously they had received no casualties with most of the Indonesian fire going high, they claimed to have hit a number. Whichever way there was no time to dally and having given the Pioneers about five minutes to get into position I ordered the Reconnaissance Platoon to withdraw by bounds keeping the enemy under constant fire. This proved to be a difficult manoeuvre since the riflemen were widely spread and coordination was difficult. A young Lance Corporal called Birbahadur was an absolute tower of strength rushing from threatened sector to sector directing fire and shouting encouragement. The real Section Commander, a man of great promise in peace was nowhere to be seen having taken cover behind a tree. He was subsequently branded a coward and his career ended, yet

Lance Corporal Birbahadur Pun DCM
*… as an absolute tower of strength rushing from threatened sector
to sector directing fire and shouting encouragement*

how natural an impulse is self preservation?

Once the Reconnaissance Platoon were clear I rejoined the Anti Tank Platoon who were still engaged in a furious but inconclusive fire fight with the enemy on the other side of the river. Since the Indonesians didn't seem to have grasped the fact that the Reconnaissance Platoon had departed I seized my opportunity and got the Anti Tanks out of the ambush and back to the strongpoint where I found Bhagtasing had arranged the Pioneers into a tight perimeter behind the two fallen trees. Grabbing two GPMG gun teams from the Anti Tank Platoon to thicken up the defence of the strongpoint I sent both the Reconnaissance Platoon and the Anti Tanks back to the ambush base because that was now the vital area. All the while the Indonesians kept firing at us and mortaring the area but it seemed from the direction of their fire that they still thought we were in the ambush position.

I was just beginning to congratulate myself on extricating ourselves from a nasty situation when Corporal Bhagtasing told me that he had been unable to find the checkpoint party on his way back to the strongpoint. The obvious answer was that they had withdrawn with the Anti Tanks or Reconnaissance to the ambush base but a check on the radio to the withdrawing platoons confirmed that this was not the case. Whilst wrestling with this problem we heard crashing about in the thick bushes and moments later the Indonesians attacked. I didn't really see much more than moving blurred figures twisting in and out through the bushes and then the concerted hammering of our machine guns, screams, shouts of command, bullets flicking and whining and then it was all over and the Indonesians had withdrawn. The problem of our missing checkpoint party remained. Their disappearance filled me with frustration since now was an ideal moment to withdraw but I couldn't leave without them accounted for. It suddenly occurred to me that they were probably lying somewhere close pinned down by fire from friend and foe alike. In a moment of crass stupidity I told Bhagtasing to look after things and vaulted over the fallen tree and slithered down the small slope into the thick jungle below. After shouting the name of the Sergeant Major I saw two figures in jungle green approach, elated I beckoned to them, they were Indonesians! Almost as surprised as I they hesitated before shooting. Three shots rang out from behind me, the Indonesians went to ground and a frenzied voice shouted 'Aunu come!' – behind me. Together we dashed back to the safety of the perimeter -- moments later another attack surged in from whence we had just come and Corporal Bhagtasing's machine guns broke it up as before. I looked then at my deliverer, one Rifleman Hariprasad Gurung of the Assault Pioneers. On his own initiative he had followed me – he, whom according to his Platoon Commander, had never shown any initiative in anything before. Why? I put my arm round his shoulders and hugged him, words were unnecessary.

This latest attack convinced me that we had to get out quickly as it was just a matter of time before the Indonesians had the sense to get behind us and cut off our withdrawal. I got onto Battalion HQ and asked to speak to Colonel Nick. He came onto the set almost immediately. In a few sentences I told him the situation and left him with the decision. As ever with Colonel Nick there was no dithering; his calm orders for me to get all the company into the ambush base without delay brooked no argument. A few seconds later Surendraman got on the radio from the firm base and reported the Reconnaissance and Anti Tank Platoons safely in base together with the Gurkha medical orderly from the checkpoint party. If one was back I hoped that the others might trickle in.

I then ordered Bhagtasing to get his Pioneers back keeping one light machine gun in position to the last.

Just as the last of the Pioneers was making his way into the swamp we again heard the tell tale crashing of bushes and shouted orders. The Light Machine Gunner Lance Corporal Reshambahadur Thapa ran back up the hill, saw that the Indonesians had reached the logs and gripping his gun to his waist fired off a complete magazine to the accompaniment of more screams and shouts. In the resulting confusion we slunk back into the safety of the dark and dank swamp

Lance Corporal Resambahdur Thapa MM
... Gripping his gun to his waist fired off a complete
magazine to the accompaniment of more screams and shouts...

leaving behind the howls of wounded, shouted orders, and the acrid smell of cordite hanging in the air.

As we returned to our firm base I could clearly hear the Indonesians starting to follow up in the swamp behind us. I knew that providing we could reach our ambush base without being cut off we would be alright since it was sited in a natural commanding position and well defended with trenches, mines and cleared fields of fire. Accordingly we moved as fast as we could and in about ten minutes arrived back within the perimeter.

As the returning soldiers arranged their ammunition in their slit trenches Surendraman briefed me on the defence plan after which Sergeant Major Smith explained to me the artillery fire plan he had worked out for the defence of the base and the harassment of the Indonesians now closing in on it. For a moment I hesitated about bringing down shell fire when we still had men unaccounted for in the area where the shells would fall. Although a harsh decision it was not a difficult one for we desperately needed the artillery to break up any Indonesian attack and so I told Sergeant Major Smith to get on with his fire plan. He had showed great initiative. Realising that with the Artillery Officer missing there was nobody to coordinate and fire the guns he did it himself having the necessary skill to do so as most SAS have. Moments later came the comforting crump of our own artillery in front of us. We stayed on in the base for one hour by which time it became clear from enemy signal shots that they were working their way between us and the border. Nevertheless I was most unwilling to leave the area before at least we had carried out one more final search for our missing men whom I was convinced were still close and alive and not in Indonesian hands. I therefore got hold of Colonel Nick on the radio, appraised him of the situation and told him of my intention to covertly approach the ambush area with a fighting patrol to try and locate the missing men. This he would not agree stressing that the most important thing was to extricate the company before the Indonesians closed the net between us and the border. Thus it was with heavy heart but a certain relief that I led the company silently down into the swamp towards the border. We went back a different way but all through the afternoon we could hear Indonesian signal shots to the rear of us. We moved very quickly only pausing for a short stop to make radio contact with Battalion HQ to hear the glad news that the missing signaller had been picked up at the gun position on the border covered in blood and incoherent. We had already questioned the medical orderly who had been part of the checkpoint group but all he could say was that he got separated from the rest of the checkpoint group during the fighting on the flanks and had withdrawn with the Reconnaissance Platoon. The news about the signaller didn't however bode very well for either Captain John Masters or the Company Sergeant Major.

By late afternoon we were close to the border and the painstaking approach march of five days had been covered in six hours. The men were very tired after a week of marching and fighting and so when we heard two shots fired close to Kandai hill a feeling of overwhelming exhaustion heavily negated my desire to deal with an enemy who it appeared had got to the border first. However after an hour's searching we could find nothing so we pushed on to the Kandai gun position arriving just before dusk fell.

Here a strange tale greeted us. Apparently the shots had been fired by our lost Artillery Captain John Masters who had wanted to alert the attention of those on the gun position. He had come back to the border to get help having left a badly wounded Company Sergeant Major somewhere in the swamp having carried him away from the area of fighting. 'D' Company had been helicoptered up and John had now gone off with them to find him. Tired as I was I realised that 'D' Company would never find the lost man and that the only way to get him back alive would be for myself and some picked men from Support Company to go off and search because we knew the area. John Masters could probably remember the place where he had left Hariprasad but would not be able to get there. I then appraised Colonel Nick of my intentions and after some persuasion he agreed.

Sipping Mortar Platoon rum with Surendraman we chose eighteen of our best men, our two best scouts, Ramparsad and Birkhabahadur, our best machine gunners including the indomitable Resembahadur, our brightest and strongest noncommissioned officers and of course Surendraman and Sergeant Major Smith of the SAS

Chapter 6

After a fitful sleep we set off just after dawn and by 8.30 we had caught up a slow moving 'D' Company paused for brewing tea. Accepting a cup I sat down with John Masters and Piers Erskine-Tullock commanding 'D' Company and planned how best to extricate our wounded Sergeant Major. John looked completely washed out after his ordeal and unbeknown at the time was ill with scrub typhus which would put him in hospital for many weeks. Slowly and unemotionally he told us what had happened.

As soon as he heard firing he radioed back to the gun position telling them simply 'Contact -- wait out' whilst he checked on his map in case we wanted fire brought down on the Indonesians rather than their suspected mortar positions to the north. At that moment a group of Indonesians came round the back of the ambush and started shooting at them. Sad to say the medical orderly ran for his life whilst the Sergeant Major and John shot back. Meanwhile fighting was general throughout the ambush so nobody was aware of the checkpoint group's plight. During this exchange of shots the Sergeant Major was hit by five sub machine gun bullets in the leg and thigh and could not walk. John therefore decided to carry him back towards the strongpoint where he knew the company would eventually return. Unfortunately John's sense of direction played him false and instead of going to the strongpoint he went south of the ambush back to the river. He ordered the Signaller, a young Gurkha Lance Corporal called Tekbahadur to help him with Hariprasad but the Gurkha refused to leave the checkpoint. Before John could coerce him more Indonesians appeared and charged; the Signaller shot one who collapsed dead on top of him, thus his blood soaked uniform. After this the Signaller became separated from John and the wounded Sergeant Major and ditching his radio set headed back towards the border.

Meanwhile John dragging the wounded Sergeant Major encountered the river and realising his mistake took a compass bearing and headed towards the border, carrying the wounded Hariprasad on his back. He hoped that his bearing might cross the company's withdrawal route. At this time he could hear nobody except the Indonesians and felt that we had pulled back, although in fact we were searching for him at the checkpoint. Having carried the Sergeant Major for another hundred yards or so he heard renewed firing to his north which was actually the fighting round the strongpoint. However since he had no idea what the ultimate fate of the company had been he felt it best to go on for as long as he could towards the border.

Thus passed for him what must have been a ghastly few hours as he half pulled, half carried the groaning Sergeant Major through the mud and slime of the swamp expecting at any time to be discovered by the Indonesians who were not noted for the quality of mercy.

I asked him if he had heard us shouting for him but all he could remember was the shouts and orders of the

Indonesians and finally a very long burst of machine gun fire followed by yells and shots. This must have been Resambahadur's action on the strongpoint.

Eventually he reached the river at Aachen and realising he couldn't get the Sergeant Major across he chose a prominent tree and made him as comfortable as he could under it, changing the field dressing he had so hastily put on when the man was first wounded. Then leaving his water bottles with Hariprasad he swam the river and headed back to the sound of the gun which was still covering our withdrawal. The rest we knew.

Since 'D' Company did not know the area and were carrying full packs I suggested that we lead, taking John Masters with us whilst they covered our rear. With 'D' Company was Howard Manuel, the doctor, who was now getting his 'High Noon' for real. Major Piers Erskine Tulloch who commanded 'D' Company was happy to fall in with this idea so I went back to Surendraman and calling in Sergeant Major Smith and our scouts, we worked out how best to tackle the problem. Our plan was for John Masters to lead for as long as he recognised his track from yesterday thereafter he would hand over to our scouts. Unfortunately it had rained hard during the night so I was not very sanguine about our chances of picking up his tracks.

After about half an hour's walking John lost his route and the scouts took over. John had behaved with the most amazing gallantry but was now totally exhausted and drained. Our only hope now was the skill of two young Gurkhas Lance Corporal Ramparsad Gurung and Lance Corporal Birkhabahadur Gurung. In this mass of primeval forest and swamp they had to find one man's tracks in the soft ground.

Quietly, patiently they padded across our front as helplessly we watched them, knowing a man's life swayed in the balance. An hour passed and still they had found nothing -- we were all close to despair. John himself sat hunched half conscious of what was going on.

Suddenly there was a soft whistle -- they had found the tracks! Throughout that long day the two scouts traced the tracks. They often lost them but always picked them up again using as their markers tiny bruises on leaves and bent twigs and the smallest indentation in the ground. By late afternoon they had traced the tracks to the river and John confirmed it as the place where he had crossed. I felt like kneeling down in the mud and giving thanks but there were more pressing matters to attend to.

Leaving 'D' Company to protect the river crossing we took the by now exhausted Howard Manuel across the river to where the Sergeant Major lay more dead than alive in the roots of a vast black barked tree. The smell of his wound made us uneasy. Howard Manuel, overcoming his exhaustion from this unwonted exertion, expertly examined his wounds and pronounced that unless he was got to medical care by nightfall he would lose his leg through gangrene.

As the rules of 'Claret' operations stood, we were obliged to carry him back across the border which would take us at least twenty-four hours through thick jungle, by which time he would probably be dead; his only hope was a helicopter. After a talk with Piers and Howard we called Colonel Nick to the radio and Howard spoke to him direct. Colonel Nick didn't hesitate and told us to be ready to receive a helicopter in two hours. We were to make a hole in the jungle canopy big enough to winch down a stretcher.

Then followed a period of intense activity as 'D' Company hitherto relegated to a somewhat passive role started to hack down the jungle on a small hillock chosen by Sergeant Major Smith as the best spot to carry out a winching operation. We had only two hours before dusk. 'D' Company throwing all caution to the winds hacked at the jungle in frenzy with saw and kukri. Meanwhile with painstaking slowness we bore the wounded Sergeant Major across the river and through the jungle, with four men clearing the way in front, four carrying the improvised stretcher and the rest of us carrying the eight men's weapons and equipment.

After about an hour we joined up with 'D' Company. Piers, their commander stood arms akimbo whilst all round trees crashed to the ground. Creeping around the jungle in a stealthy way never really commended itself to Piers, he was much more in his element now and would have welcomed an Indonesian attack to complete his satisfaction. Here amongst the crashing trees and darkening sky he would surely have inflicted a bloody reverse upon them, a sort of oriental Gotterdammerung!

Unfortunately the sky was darkening all too quickly and all the signs of a tropical storm threatened. We warned Battalion HQ but the helicopter had already left.

Thus it was in torrential rain amidst stabs of lightning that the Whirlwind helicopter piloted by Flight Lieutenant Brian Skillicorn arrived with a clatter of rotor blades into what despite all efforts now seemed a totally inadequate clearing. Buffeted by wind, with great courage and skill, he inexorably drove his machine into the clearing helped immensely by Sergeant Major Smith's skilled handling of the radio direction beam (SARBE); down came the stretcher

Flying Officer Brian Skillicorn RAF
With great courage and skill he inexorably drove his machine into the clearing.

and confusion, as nobody in 'D' Company knew how to put a casualty in it. Seconds ticked away whilst the helicopter swung dangerously between the trees. Sergeant Major Smith leaping over the falling trees with an agility that belied his frame unlashed the stretcher and with immense care the Sergeant Major was lain upon it – but now the helicopter shot up vertically with the stretcher desperately swinging like a cocoon below it. Thus in this rather unceremonious manner the casualty disappeared from our sight. A mixture of intense relief and weariness overcame me and I sat on a tree trunk and surveyed the scene as though through the eyes of a total stranger. The rain now streamed down and the gathering darkness was accentuated by the pinpoints of light from 'D' Company's hexamine fires as they cooked their evening meal. There had been no time to make any base organisation or find water and all we could do was sleep where we stood. It seemed inconceivable that the Indonesians were not aware of our presence but they had so far made no move – perhaps they were waiting for the dawn or perhaps they had had enough. After all our casualty evacuation could be interpreted by them as final preparations before another border incursion? Only monitoring of our radio net could have given them the true situation and since they had few if any Nepali speakers this was denied them.

I knew I had to get up off the tree trunk and make decisions, go and plan with Piers, check that John Masters was OK, thank Sergeant Major Smith for his splendid help and talk to my Support Company men but this langour of exhaustion insidiously delayed me. As so often in the past it was Surendraman whose quiet sense came to the fore. Quietly he came up from the darkness and asked me for my water bottle mug. This he filled a third full with rum from one of his water bottles and together we drank in silence. As if understanding my concerns he laid them to rest one by one; John Masters was asleep having been cared for by my orderly, Piers has sent a message saying we should stand-to a good hour before dawn and move off back to the border as soon as it got light, us leading and them covering our rear.

As for the men, apart from the sentries out in the gloom they were gathered round the flickering flames of a couple of hexamine cookers, the light playing softly on strong open faces, scarred hands and the occasional bared chest of a soldier despairing of wet and filthy clothes and preferring dry skin. That almost emotional warmth of companionship-in-arms caught at my throat for the tired but successful remnant of my company. Even the usually taciturn and wholly self reliant Sergeant Major Smith was affected and breaking the silence he said to me 'They are some of the best and I've been with a good few!'

What matter a quarter of a mess tin of soggy rice and a wet groundsheet in the mud; we had come through.

We were all awake before dawn, damp shivering muscles stiff and unresponsive. Crouched behind trees we awaited that gradual lightening that in the jungle passes for sunrise.

After stand-to I went over to Piers wending my way through the 'D' Company soldiers exchanging with them the odd joke or remark. Gurkhas like British soldiers are amazingly insular, and a man in Support Company would view another company as a totally alien environment. Occasionally soldiers had to be posted from one company to another generally for career reasons and they always anticipated such moves with dread! I found Piers busy laying on our helicopter lift surrounded by tea, shaving kit, signals pads etc whilst his orderly endeavoured to induce him to leave the radio and shave whilst the water was hot. His burly frame and bluff but genuine demeanour stamped a veneer of normality on our situation and made me aware of my ten day growth of beard and ripped and stinking clothes. Since it was obvious that it would be some time before 'D' Company packed we agreed that Support Company should go back with John Masters to the border and catch the first lift of helicopters.

Thanking Piers for all his help I went back to my men who

were ready to go having only had to fold their poncho capes. John Masters was swaying with fever so with Bhimbahadur my orderly helping him we set off and by 10.00 we were on the gun position waiting for our helicopters.

The warmth of direct sun came as a benison of delight and sitting down around the landing zone, we revelled in Mortar Platoon tea and biscuits brought to us by smiling cheery recruits agog to hear our tale. Almost too soon came the distant clunk of helicopter rotor blades and grabbing our packs which we had left on the LZ two nights ago we formed up into sticks ready to emplane.

Colonel Nick was on the Lundu LZ to meet us; obviously delighted at the outcome. Taking the Platoon Commanders, Lance Corporal Birbahadur and John Masters with me we crushed into the Colonel's room to tell him of the operation.

The Colonel had a tale as well. The night after our battle his radio intercept had picked up from Indonesian military radio traffic that they had captured a British officer and a Gurkha NCO and were sending them down river to Siluas by boat. Thus Colonel Nick had hardly believed his luck when John Masters had turned up at the LZ. Later I heard that Colonel Nick had ordered the helicopter to pick Hariprasad up on his own initiative and had been in it swinging above the trees last night. Thus had started his dispute with the Brigadier who whilst accepting the need for a helicopter had reminded the Colonel forcibly of the political policy not to send helicopters over the border.

After the others had gone Colonel Nick took me aside and said how well the company had done. He wanted me to write citations for those whom I felt deserved medals except for John Masters whose citation he would write himself.

Tomorrow we were to fly to Brigade and visit the Sergeant Major in Kuching Hospital and I was to brief the Brigadier on our action. Apparently the Indonesians had admitted to a number of casualties.

All this plethora of happy endings rather disturbed me and I felt that such hubris most inevitably lead to some ghastly nemesis on our next operation. On my way out of the Operations Room Norman Corbett told me that five of my men were being flown to Kuching Hospital that afternoon with scrub typhus – so the mites had done their work. Of those bitten only old Surendraman had not succumbed; perhaps it was the nicotine!

After I had visited the sick men, who had lost pounds, and decided our future programme with Surendraman I felt ready for a wash, shave and a substantial meal. Sitting on my bed I pulled one boot off and the next I knew it was dark. Two hours of unconsciousness had separated the taking off of two boots!

That evening Captain Surendraman had invited me to supper in the Gurkha Officers Mess. Thus it was after a delicious curry that we fell to discussing the last operation.

Inevitably conversation turned to how many casualties we had inflicted on the Indonesians. It was very difficult to be precise since only the Signaller had actually seen a dead Indonesian, although many had been seen to fall. This in itself was not surprising given the thick jungle in which we were fighting and the fact that we had been withdrawing.

In the first instance the Reconnaissance Platoon had opened fire at a range of about fifteen yards on the lead Indonesian platoon filing along the track. They claimed to have hit a number and seen them fall. However since the first thing a soldier does when fired at is to hit the deck this didn't really mean much. On the other hand it was inconceivable that they had hit nobody given that the Gurkhas were good shots, the short opening range and the fact that a light machine gun was used as well as a number of other weapons. We felt that at least six Indonesians had been hit in this first engagement. Of the next two we could be more certain since they took cover behind a tree at the foot of which was a Claymore mine. When this was detonated both were blown into the river. As Sergeant Major Smith said subsequently '. . . and that stopped them farting in church'. In the fighting round the checkpoint both John Masters and the Signaller claimed to have killed at least an Indonesian apiece at close range. As for the very heavy fire fight as the Reconnaissance Platoon withdrew and the repulse of the various Indonesian attacks on the strongpoint it was difficult to be precise; certainly they had taken casualties but how many and whether killed or wounded was difficult to say. In the end we claimed seventeen enemy casualties which the company thought far too low an estimate! Subsequently we heard that our radio intercept had picked up an Indonesian signal on the evening of the engagement which admitted to six dead and a number of wounded. Given a general average of four dead for every twelve wounded in our type of encounter battle this was probably quite near the mark although for obvious reasons they tended to understate. As for the wounded, one wouldn't give much for their chances; a combination of poor medical facilities and a six hour boat trip to their hospital in Siluas would kill many of them.

A number of lessons came out of the operation. Firstly, and

one we already knew, was that the ambush was easily the best way to damage the Indonesians. Had we been in the right place we would have killed twenty four Indonesians for there was no escape for them from a boat ambush. Secondly the importance of all round defence in the ambush which subsequently led us to favour a triangular layout with the checkpoint at the apex. Thirdly was higher formation coordination. Unbeknown to us at the time the SAS were also ambushing close by and another group had ambushed two boat loads elsewhere on the Sentimo shortly before we got into ambush. As a result of all this activity the Indonesians were clearly determined to clear the area before trying to use the river again. Whether their clearance operation that led to our engagement was prompted by SAS activity or whether they had seen us the previous day we shall never know. Either way we and the SAS should have been coordinated rather more carefully.

The last lesson was an obvious one but desperately important. We had trained and practised for the operation extensively. Every man had been aware of the overall concept and the plan in so far as it affected him. There was a clearly understood contingency plan if the ambush was taken in the flank. Thus despite an unexpected sequence of events the contingency plan worked and the company basically achieved its aim of disrupting the Indonesian line of communication.

As for the Indonesians they failed to maintain the initiative and cut off and destroy Support Company. To do so was certainly within their means but they dissipated their advantage by pressing attacks on an area they knew to be well defended. Had they instead by-passed the strongpoint and engaged the soldiers endeavouring to get back to the ambush base there could have been a very different ending. As ever the soldiers showed an aggressive spirit but poor shooting, sterile tactics and weak leadership meant that they were unable to inflict a definite tactical defeat upon us.

The next day I flew to Kuching with the Colonel and after visiting the wounded Sergeant Major in hospital we were ushered in to the Brigadier's office. A tall, strongly built man with a balding head and cheerful demeanour he did not look like a man destined to die of cancer some three years later. At his bidding I explained the operation after which he gave me a mild rebuke for not having positioned more men in the checkpoint. I was astounded, although I did my best not to show it; as for Colonel Nick he remained grimly silent. I suppose I thought I was going to be congratulated but that aside the Brigadier's conclusion seemed at the time a facile one. Each ambush had to be deployed differently but a common factor was that the firepower had to be in the shop window and men couldn't really be spared for the very unlikely eventuality of an attack on the checkpoint. That one had to leave it lightly defended was a risk that one took with all the other attendant risks of discovery and destruction. Anyway our adoption of a triangular formation was actually a better solution since it achieved the same result for no additional manpower.

Colonel Nick had other business to transact in the HQ and since our helicopter was not due until early evening I went out into the town on the pretext of doing some shopping.

Kuching was a quaint rather ramshackle town of wooden buildings on stilts with corrugated tin roofs. In it dwelt a mixed population of Chinese, Dyaks, Malays and Ibans living closely but individually their differing lifestyles. I found a bench overlooking the tidal river bank and enjoyed the complete and calming luxury of just watching the world go by. The long boats slicing through the muddy water powered by outboards whilst more stately sampans chugged here and there moving bales of merchandise from heavily loaded lighters. By an old ruined warehouse a massive bougainvillea covered everything in a purple cascade whilst the smell of frangipani mixed with that of cooking and spices from the busy streets. Malay girls, their shapely flanks tightly swathed in gaily coloured sarongs padded flatfoot in the dusty streets. Here was a world full of colour, life and variety so different to the vast expanse of swampy jungle that had become our environment in all its unknown danger both from man and nature. Like a prisoner on parole all too soon the hands of my watch edged towards the time of return. With some reluctance I headed back to the realities of Confrontation and meeting up with Colonel Nick we flew back to Lundu with the evening sun lighting up mangrove swamp and jungle.

The next few days were the first of real rest for a very long time. Whilst I wrote up operational reports and citations in my attap roofed office Surendraman pressed on with sorting out the lately neglected administration of the company and the integration of the new recruits into the platoons. With no cross border operation in the offing we were able to concentrate on essential training such as weapon handling, shooting and first aid of which the operational soldier can never have enough. At the doctor's instigation and with our recent experiences to the fore each soldier was given an individual first aid kit in a tobacco tin. It consisted of a phial of morphine with syringe, two purple hearts and some tetracycline tablets. The idea was that if a soldier should become separated from the company on operations and be wounded he could inject himself with morphine to kill the pain and so perhaps continue walking towards the border. The tetracycline would slow gangrene from setting in and the purple hearts would have a similar effect as morphine for lesser wounds and injuries. Again remembering our last operation we bought a simple tin compass for every man to help them get back over the border if lost.

During the close quarter fighting of our last operation I had been struck by the relative lack of firepower available to small groups fighting on their own. As a result I got the armourer to file down part of the rifle trigger mechanism to allow it to fire automatic if required. This done we laid on a demonstration for a rather dubious Colonel Nick who still held strongly to the old Indian army maxim of one shot one man. However whilst this was all very well for when you could clearly see your man it was not quite so suitable for confused close quarter fighting in thick jungle. After a successful demonstration the Colonel agreed to two such rifles being adapted in each section which considerably enhanced the company's firepower.

This period of relative calm was soon curtailed when five days after returning from our last operation the call to arms came again. It was about 5.00 in the evening and I was just pulling off my boots after all day on the jungle range. My orderly came in and told me I was wanted in the Operations Room. Wearily I pulled my boots on again and with muttered curses repaired to the Commissioner's House.

John Parkes then briefed me that a police report had just

Gunong Gadang where we searched for the communist terrorists

been received concerning a group of twenty armed CCO terrorists (Communist Clandestine Organisation) who had been seen on the Sematon road near Kampong Serayan and we were to go and find them and bring them to book.

Since there was only about two hours before nightfall this was rather a tall order so I decided to send the Reconnaissance Platoon out that night to see if they could find anything with the rest of the company following next morning.

There followed one of the most protracted operations the company had been involved in. The area concerned could only have been five square miles or so but the main Gunong Gadang feature was three thousand feet high and its sides were covered in very thick jungle often growing out of sheer rock. The Reconnaissance Platoon's initial search proved fruitless and by dawn I had the rest of the company moving out to join them. After a chat with Sergeant Chabilal of the Reconnaissance Platoon on the road close to Kampong Serayan I split the foothills nearest the road in three sectors for each platoon to search. This we did all day but it was like looking for a needle in a haystack. That night we were recalled and briefed up for a much larger operation to search the complete Gunong Gadang area with a company of 1st Battalion 7th Gurkhas and a company of 1st Battalion 10th Gurkhas who were to be flown in at first light the next morning. As home team we were given the peak area of Gunong Gadang, all three thousand feet of it!

Chapter 7

14 SEPTEMBER – 1 OCTOBER 1965

At about 9.00 the next morning having met in the foothills with Garry Johnson the 10th Gurkha Company Commander we set off on our long climb up Gunong Gadang with a platoon of 'B' Company to give us added strength to cover as wide an area as possible. It was a desperately steep climb carrying our hundred or so pounds of equipment through thick jungle on a slippery path, and by the time we got to the top even the supremely fit Gurkha soldiers were wet with perspiration. We were not alone on top of the mountain for here in the coolness and cloud worked the Signal Platoon radio rebroadcast station. Their task was to pick up radio transmissions from company bases and patrols and rebroadcast them through to Battalion HQ. They lived on top of this hill without relief for a month at a time and this morning a light Sioux helicopter had come in with the barber to cut their hair. Whilst the company brewed tea I repaired to the barber musing that few men could have climbed so far for a haircut.

The next five days saw the company searching minutely but inconclusively amongst the jungle covered crest of the Gunong Gadang feature. We were looking for some sign of human habitation or movement; broken foliage, parang cuts, footmarks; for a cigarette butt or empty can would have been too much to hope for.

At the end of five days' fruitless searching we returned to Lundu to collect another ten days rations to continue the search. I was quite glad to get back as a huge boil had erupted at the back of my leg and walking was very painful. As we trudged back I realised that this was the last operation that I would do with Captain Surendraman who was due to return to Nepal for six months leave after well over the statutory three years service. I realised how much I had relied on his support and advice and how greatly I had enjoyed his companionship and humour. His departure would deprive me of a completely unbiased and balanced sounding board for all manner of problems and the nearer we got to Lundu the sadder I became.

In the event we spent two days at Lundu which was enough to get my leg pumped full of penicillin and to give Surendraman a quiet send off, although not the proper party that we had planned.

News percolated through that the 1/7th Gurkha ambush had found a CCO hideout in a cave, capturing a young Chinaman believed to be a courier. He was brought down the hill by an escort party and then put in a Scout helicopter to be flown to Kuching for interrogation. A big Gurkha from the Mechanical Transport Platoon went with him in the helicopter as escort. Five minutes out of Lundu the helicopter crashed killing both of them and the pilot in rather mysterious circumstances. It seemed unlikely that a rather diminutive Chinese youth should have overpowered his escort and crashed the helicopter into the river. I was inclined to believe that a sudden power failure to which the Scout helicopter was then prone might have been to blame.

Either way the only hopeful lead to the CCO gang had been silenced and a cheerful father of two and driver of heavy trucks had gone with him.

That evening I was called up to the Operations Room and Norman Corbett briefed me to take over the 1/7 GR ambush near to the cave they had discovered. That night we had the film 'Some Like it Hot' in the Mess. Marilyn Monroe's nubile warmth and sexuality reminded me of the deprivation of my present life. Strangely enough the soldiers were less vulnerable in this respect since most of them were married and anyhow they were not bound by such narrow moral boundaries as were we their officers. They married young for mainly economic gain, slept in many other beds without guilt or anguish and ended up contentedly with their wives working the dusty hill soil of Nepal.

Next morning I sent the company under Lieutenant Nandaraj on to take over the 1/7 GR ambush whilst I attended a promotion conference. These occasions generally developed into a slanging match between opposing Company Commanders trying to push their own men into the limited vacancies. Fortunately we had in John Parkes a quite exceptional Adjutant and despite his comparative lack of seniority he held the conference on a tight rein. Our recent successes helped our promotion prospects and as I trudged up the Gunong Gadang yet again with my orderly and signaller I had every reason to be satisfied with the results. On joining the company I found that 1/7 GR had already left so letting Nandaraj set the ambush I went and rested prior to doing the night ambush.

On the second day towards evening Nandaraj captured a Chinese woman and child carrying rice up to the cave. The woman was short, thick set and featureless but the child was sweet with a lively intelligent face now sullied by misery and tears. They had obviously been resupplying the terrorists and word had not yet got to them that the hiding place had been discovered. We cheered them up with orange juice and biscuits and then sent them down to the road under escort. The cave that the terrorists had been using was by a small stream and was very well organised with a cooking and sleeping area.

After two more days ambushing I was told to cordon and search one of the farms at the foot of Gunong Gadang feature at dawn. Apparently one of the terrorists was thought to be hiding there but after careful preparations and a very stealthy approach we drew a blank. On return, stiff and sleepless, from this abortive mission our morale was unexpectedly raised. The route to our base took us past a spectacular waterfall plunging into a deep, green cool pool. In this pool were three quite naked and very shapely Land Dayak girls. Their abandoned gaiety quite unsullied by any embarrassment made us forget our sweat, dirt and heavy equipment and we smiled and laughed with them at their spontaneous beauty and fun. All too soon the column wound into the darkness of the jungle and the sweat ran again as we toiled up the steep slope of the Gunong.

The next day I took out a patrol to search another area of the hill feature. On our way back we crossed a big stream tumbling down amongst the huge boulders. As we crossed it the sharp eyed leading scout noticed a small roll of vine on top of one of the rocks. It was of a type used for making big baskets. Looking around he saw near to the vine a large hole under a rock at the bottom of which he could just see the outline of a pair of plastic slippers.

It was clear that this was another terrorist hide so taking no chances we threw down a white phosphorous grenade to flush out anybody who might have been there. When nobody emerged I sent down a particularly diminutive rifleman to have a look round. After about ten minutes he appeared from an entirely different direction having used another exit from the cave. He told us that the cave was a big one, full of stores and possibly in current use.

On investigating the cave we found a superbly organised hiding place which but for the vine we would never have found. One part of the cave had been dug into huge shelves, the lower ones with blankets for sleeping and the upper ones for storage. The storage area was full of tins of chicken and pork and sacks of rice, whilst further down the exit tunnel part of the stream flowed through and here vegetables were kept fresh on a ledge by the running water. We found no weapons but quite a lot of 9mm ammunition as well as pamphlets and diaries in Mandarin script.

My first reaction was admiration for these young Chinese communists who, despairing of ever achieving fair opportunities in a Malay state, had taken to arms. They were clearly well organised and hardy.

After another four days in ambush Colonel Nick called us back and so, gutting the caves of anything of value, we staggered down to the road carrying our enormous burdens. Just short of the road there was a small stream and one of the youngest soldiers recently arrived from recruit training slipped whilst negotiating it and crashed to the ground, terrorist rice spilling everywhere. The look of surprise and hurt pride on his young face made us all laugh and I reflected how close and happy a team we were.

It was sheer joy to be going back to Lundu with its seemingly utopian comforts after so long in the jungle and the soldiers echoed their joy singing carefree Nepalese songs as the trucks raced along the dusty road home.

The gang of twenty whom we were seeking never really recovered from the destruction of their hideout and following an informer tip off a month or so later 'B' Company captured some of them and killed one trying to escape.

On arrival back having checked in to the Operations Room I showered and having changed into clean clothes I strolled over to the Mess for a cold beer and a read of the English newspapers.

On my way I bumped into Major Johnny Lawes the Battalion Second in Command who ascertaining that it was just past noon decided to join me. For a few minutes I told him about our various operations in which he took an immense interest not least because he had been the previous Company Commander and I one of his Platoon Commanders. His job as Battalion Second in Command involved him in spending half his time in Singapore looking after the battalion rear party, barracks and families. As such he was able to give me all the wives' gossip and the happenings in Singapore.

Starved of such conversation it made good listening especially the saga of Colonel Nick's cat. This large bushy and rather plump feline was the apple of Nick and his wife Margaret's eyes. Unfortunately the much beloved had become sick so Margaret had promptly whisked it into Singapore in the Colonel's staff car for treatment. The treatment had necessitated several visits which the Gurkha staff car driver had painstakingly annotated in the work ticket as 'Visit of Commanding Sahib's cat for medic treatment'. With the Motor Transport Officer with the battalion in Borneo there was nobody to expunge this masterpiece before it ascended higher to the Defence Auditor or whoever reads these things. As a result some desperately zealous staff officer in HQ Far East Land Forces started ringing Johnny up threatening him with all sorts of investigations into misuse of army transport. Knowing Johnny I suspect he got fairly short shrift!

After ordering another cold 'Tiger' beer Johnny fixed me with his disconcertingly quizzical gaze and said 'You *do* know you are *supposed* to be in charge of the Warrant Officers' and Sergeants' Mess accounts here in Lundu don't you?'

In those days it was customary for young officers in Gurkha regiments to take on the supervision and ultimate responsibility for one account. I had drawn the Sergeants' Mess account which was known to be in chaos before we ever went to Lundu from Singapore. I had protested strongly on the grounds that I would be on operations most of the time but had been overruled. In taking over this type of account one hoped to have the assistance of some able Mess Treasurer so that apart from the odd cash and stock check he virtually ran the account. My misfortune was to have drawn the most chaotic Treasurer imaginable. His idea of accounting was to muster the successive day's takings in little piles on top of the roof rafters. I had soon realised that I would have to get a massive grip on matters lest there be a financial 'gulmal' of fairly awe inspiring dimensions. The problem was that so intense had been operations that I simply hadn't had the time to put matters right or even work out how I might do so.

Apparently Johnny, in his efficient way, had brought over the Paymaster from Singapore to check all the accounts with predictable results. There was nothing for it but to make a clean breast, conscious that financial irregularity and mucking around with fellow officers' wives had put paid to more young officers' careers than I cared to remember.

The upshot was that much to my relief some other poor unfortunate was given the account whilst I got away with a ticking off. Actually things weren't quite as bad as they might have been as when all the little piles on the roof rafters of the Mess office were counted up they came to fairly much what they should have done. As Johnny subsequently mentioned, his magisterial rebuke was somewhat softened by Colonel Nick saying he didn't really care as long as Support Company were killing Indonesians!

Chapter 8

20 OCTOBER – 2 NOVEMBER 1965

Much to Colonel Nick's annoyance the Government had temporarily suspended 'Claret' operations but this did not inhibit him from planning for the day when restrictions would be lifted.

Thus it came as no great surprise to me to be called into his lair and given the outline of a two company operation with 'A' Company scheduled for mid October and known as 'Monsoon Drain'. In outline it consisted of a repeat of our previous operation on the River Sentimo using twice the number of men split into two company ambushes. I was not very happy about the idea since I felt that the Indonesians were probably taking precautions against such operations by active river line patrolling and something rather more original might be needed.

As soon as the border restriction was lifted at the end of the first week of October planning started in earnest. I flew over to Biawak to talk the thing through with Major Len Lauderdale who commanded 'A' Company.

Biawak was the first of the purpose-built strongpoint bases. It was situated almost on the border having been moved from its original position alongside the village of Biawak. On the day I visited it was still under construction and I saw the huge bunkers designed by a certain Major

Bowen of the Royal Engineers. Eventually the whole base was to be underground with the soldiers safe against surprise mortar attacks from the Indonesian base of Sadjingan some three miles over the other side of the border. In this huge base 'A' and 'D' Companies lived supported by a 105 Pack Howitzer dug into a vast circular pit. I always rather felt for the soldiers since as soon as they got back from cross border operations they went straight back to digging their fortifications.

The plan I developed with Len was for us both to cross the border at a single entry point and then once within striking distance of the Sentimo for me to swing north and ambush close to Babang Baba whilst he ambushed the river join further south. Once we were both in position we hoped that an ambush in one area would lead to reinforcements being moved by boat which could then be ambushed by the other company. The plan was simple and had worked before. For this operation I had been given a platoon from 'C' Company so our total strength for the operation was about two hundred.

On return to Lundu I found that the border restriction was on again so since it was the main Gurkha religious festival of Dashera that week I told Lieutenant Nandaraj who was now acting as my Second in Command to let the company get on with their festivities. They needed no second bidding, and every night was spent watching Nepalese song and dance routines for which the younger and more graceful soldiers dressed as women, and very convincing they looked! These dances were interspersed with comic turns which irreverently mocked all aspects of the military establishment and invariably included an irascible Brigadier and a helicopter.

On the day of 'Mar' all the weapons were stacked and hung with flowers and then two goats were sacrificed and their blood traced in a circle round the garlanded weapons. This traditional religious appeasement assumed a marked significance in my mind since the weapons had already been used in anger and were soon to be used again.

As luck would have it the end of Dashera coincided with the lifting of the Border restriction and we were warned to start the operation on the 20th of October.

As we started our normal operation run-in of weapon and radio testing, practices on the jungle range and ambush and patrol formations, a recurrence of my old fever flared up so that the day before the operation I had to go to bed. This created a great fuss and Len Lauderdale flew over from Biawak to find out what was going on.

Next morning although I felt totally drained of energy the fever seemed to have abated. Whilst waiting for the helicopters to lift us out (so much of a soldier's life seems to be spent waiting for helicopters) Norman Corbett came down to the Landing Zone to tell me that a very nice policeman called Bob Graver had been killed attacking an Indonesian camp. The story was all a bit confused but it transpired that, upset by various slurs on the effectiveness of the mainly Iban Police Field Force, he organised an attack on a well fortified Indonesian base. Bereft of supporting fire this was obviously a very hazardous undertaking unless complete surprise could be achieved; it wasn't and he and others were killed during a most gallant attack.

Somewhat downcast by this news I turned back to the job in hand. The move in for the operation fortunately went reasonably well and soon our long column was across the border and into the by now familiar swamp.

Over the previous two weeks or so the monsoon rains had poured down and as a result the swamp was even deeper than on the last operation. We struggled on as best we could, but progress was agonisingly slow with a column of two hundred men. That evening we fortunately found a large low island in the swamp on which there was room for two companies to harbour. It was clear to me that we ought now to split up and go towards our separate objectives, as at present progress was too slow. Len agreed this and under a dripping poncho cape we tied up all the details. The most important detail was when to open fire as unless both companies were properly in ambush before fire was opened Indonesian reinforcements might well come up or down river without being ambushed with possibly very adverse results for us.

The next morning Support Company set off for our ambush position south of Babang Baba.

I felt very much for Lieutenant Peter Little who was accompanying us on this operation. Only a few weeks before he had been at university as a carefree undergraduate. Now he was plunged into filthy swamp jungle in wildest Indonesia; never dry, beset by mosquitoes and leeches (one of which had already got in his hair) and served by quite the worst Gurkha orderly I had ever clapped eyes on. Nevertheless throughout the whole operation which became increasingly fraught he never lost his sense of humour and sang-froid and upon this basis a long friendship was born. Perhaps most trying for him was an ignorance of what was going on as all deliberations and orders were in Nepali. I did the best I could for him in the occasional moments I had to spare from more pressing matters, but this was not really enough.

After about two hours marching we came to a drier area that seemed vaguely familiar and by midday we had reached another island in the swamp that we had used two months or so before. After a very careful look round for booby traps I moved the company into a harbour area and then sent out patrols to find the river which I know was within an hour's march. I went off with a patrol of the Reconnaissance Platoon on what I thought was the most promising bearing. In this way if my patrol did find the river I could conduct an immediate ambush reconnaissance thus saving time. Since we were only rationed for twelve days which with everything else was all that we could carry it was important to save time whenever possible.

When fairly close to the river I got a radio message from my base that 'A' Company had reached the river and had sighted an Indonesian base on the other side with soldiers bathing.

This was a real poser as 'A' Company had obviously got a very good target, but with only a reconnaissance patrol there was a limit to how much damage they could do. Additionally it would certainly take me another hour to reach the river with any of my patrols, all of which were small and spread over a large area. There was thus a danger that the whole thing could go off at half cock.

I got back to 'A' Company and suggested that they hold their fire and wait until the next morning, by which time we would be in position. This they accepted although in retrospect it might have been better had they not. Realising that time was short I called back my patrols and re-cast my plans. If 'A' Company had already found a position it was vital we got into ambush as fast as possible. There was simply not the time to reconnoitre for the best position; we would just have to push on as a company to the river and make our dispositions accordingly. If I was to brief the company on new plans, I had to have my patrols back in daylight and since so far none of them had reached the river, they had to come back. In the event the last patrol arrived back during 'stand to' after dark so I had not been a moment too soon.

Huddled over a rum with Nandaraj we pored over the air photos trying to find the best spot to ambush. Peter Little looked on meanwhile with an air of studious interest. In the pinprick light of a shaded torch we could just determine an eastward loop of the Sentimo which appeared to coincide with a bearing that gave a reasonable separation from 'A' Company.

I then gave out orders for a company approach march at best possible speed to get into ambush by 10.00 the next morning. In this manner we hoped that 'A' Company would still be able to get a good target – perhaps not soldiers bathing, but some other soft target the engagement of which would draw in reinforcements into our ambush.

I have to confess that at the time I was uneasy with the way that matters were proceeding. We were having to conform to another company's initiatives and in doing so we were casting aside our normal caution in approaching and siting an ambush position. All Support Company had recent experience as to how dangerous the Indonesians could be once they got wind of our presence and I did not believe that our greatly increased numbers in any way allowed us to take risks.

Our patrols that day had established that there was a low dry ridge just east of the river on our bearing and here I intended to drop off my harbour party to make base whilst I pressed on with the rest of the company.

In spite of all the imponderables I slept soundly as I generally did once an operation had started – it was the period back at Lundu just before setting off that made me tense and sleepless.

The 24th of October was a Sunday – not however a day of rest! As soon as we could see a few yards we were on our way – a long column of heavily laden men trudging westward.

Fortunately our route was mostly on dry land and we made good progress for about an hour when we arrived at the highest point of a low ridge. Here we dumped our packs and the base protection party under Lieutenant Nandaraj set to work immediately in laying out the defensive perimeter. After a few minutes rest I took the rest of the company down into the swamp towards the river.

Today the lead platoon was the Anti Tank Platoon and their leading scout was a thin rather stooped Lance Corporal called Asbahadur Gurung. Like all Gurkhas he was referred to by the last two figures of his regimental number – in his case ninety-nine or 'nubbe nubbe' in Nepali. 'Nubbe nubbe' had been one of the scouts instrumental in finding our wounded Sergeant Major and was a quite outstanding tracker. Although of rather unprepossessing appearance he was a very jovial and intelligent soldier who could be vastly amusing especially after a rum or two. After about an hour sloshing through deep swamp it was he who gave the urgent signal to halt followed by the thumbs down sign for enemy.

I suppose there must have been eighty men or so in the column but once the signal had percolated down they all stood immobile as if turned to stone. Soon, through the normal daytime noise of cicadas, birds and monkeys I heard the steady sloshing sound of a column making its way through swamp jungle. The situation that we all feared most had occurred and two heavily armed columns were now converging. If these were enemy then they must inevitably have the long term advantage, because however successful we were in a straight fire fight we were bound to suffer casualties which could immobilise us. We knew from our last operation that twelve soldiers were needed to get one badly wounded man through the swamp.

Some reading these lines will recall the exploits of the Chindits behind the Japanese lines for months in Burma, but that was total war with airstrips built in; strongholds to take casualties out and replacements in. Our 'Claret' operations were totally clandestine, our Government was not at war with Indonesia and would deny that any British Forces had crossed the border. As a result such operations had to be non-attributable, no prisoners, no wounded, no bodies could be left in the swamp from which the Indonesians could make political capital.

My first thought was that this unseen column was not enemy but 'A' Company wildly off bearing. However the more I thought about it the less likely such a possibility seemed. There was one such way to find out and crouching in the swamp I called 'A' Company on the radio. Mercifully they replied very quietly – the column was not 'A' Company.

If we remained silent it was possible the Indonesians could just pass us by but it was not a risk I could take and so I gave the signal for each man to take up the best fire position he could in the mud and water. To our north there was a small mound and to this I directed one of our GPMG's, realising that this extra foot or so of ground could make all the difference to the effectiveness of this weapon. Unfortunately on their way to the mound the man carrying the GPMG stumbled on a root and fell to his knees in the water; the sound of the enemy column faded and then stopped. They had heard us!

Then followed an hour's complete silence as each column waited for the other to give away its position and offer a target. Eventually the Indonesians slowly moved off to the north west, but they now knew exactly where we were. It was pointless for us to try and take up an ambush position with Indonesians in the area so I contacted 'A' Company to find out how they were faring. Their news was not good; apparently they had been seen getting into ambush by an Indonesian sentry and were pulling back to their base before the Indonesians mortared them.

Things were not going well and that night we had a three cornered radio conversation between Colonel Nick, myself and 'A' Company. Colonel Nick wanted us to try and ambush elsewhere although I was certain that now the Indonesians were on to us it was pointless hanging around waiting to be cut off. Colonel Nick prevailed and I made arrangements to meet with Len Lauderdale and 'A' Company next morning at their base to work out another plan.

That night I talked the matter over with Lieutenant Nandaraj and Peter Little and decided that our only chance of success was to ambush as far away from the present area as possible. This meant crossing the easterly Sentimo (we had now established that there were two arms of the river) and going north to ambush the larger westerly arm south of Berdjonkong. It also seemed to me to be wisest for us to lay one large single ambush since we would be strong enough together to fight our way out of any Indonesian attempt to cut us off.

Later, having given orders, Peter and I gossiped quietly as we lay under our dripping poncho capes. His civilised and intelligent conversation came as a welcome reminder of normality and took my mind off the unsatisfactory progress of an operation that seemed destined to go wrong. In retrospect one often knew when an operation would not turn out well, fortune appeared most infrequently and the general run of luck was adverse. The men knew too and sensed uncertainty.

We met up with 'A' Company at about 9.00 on a wet and chill morning.

As Len and I discussed plans the two companies sat silent and expectant on their packs, whilst outside 'A' Company's perimeter the sentries on their machine guns gazed into the gloom of the surrounding jungle. Everybody was on edge knowing that the Indonesians would be planning to settle with us now that they were aware that we were five miles or so within their borders.

Len went along with our plan and having told Colonel Nick of our intentions and been given his blessing we set off on what I knew would be a long hazardous march deeper into enemy territory.

At about 2.00 in the afternoon we hit the eastern arm of the Sentimo and, praying that no Indonesian boat traffic would interrupt us, I ordered Nandaraj and his Pioneers to bridge the river. This they did with their customary efficiency and by 4.00 both companies were safely on the other side and the bridge was being dismantled.

In the remaining hour of good light we made the best speed possible in the hope that by putting as much distance as we could between where we had last been sighted and the new ambush position we would again be able to surprise the Indonesians.

By the time we got to the ridge line I had chosen for a camp site we were all tired and there were several men down with fever. We had now been marching and counter marching in vile conditions for six days, and badly needed a little time to properly clean and check our weapons, dry out our radio sets and rest the men sick with fever.

After discussions with Len we decided to press on next day to our final base and then rest up and reorganise before ambushing the day after. I was fairly confident about finding the right area for a base since the river was clearly defined on the air photo. Also I knew exactly where we were as before crossing the easterly Sentimo we had walked through the scene of our last action in the area. Despite our need for speed I had given the column a few minutes rest whilst I walked with my orderly around the old ambush position. A broken sapling here and there and on bigger trees the sap congealed around bullet holes made me recall how fortunate we had been. Under a bush I found three full machine carbine magazines belonging to a Section Commander who, stunned by the effect of real bullets, never left the safety of his tree trunk. Fortunately his section Second in Command had risen valiantly to the occasion and had rallied his section and kept the Indonesians out of the ambush position, subsequently receiving the Distinguished Conduct Medal.

On the next day as planned we set off for our final base area, reaching it about midday, and having put out sentries we set to work preparing weapons and radios and ministering to those who were down with fevers of one sort or another.

One of our main problems was that our supply of smokeless chemical fuel was down to two days and appreciating that the longer we ambushed the more likely the Indonesians were to discover us, we decided to conserve our smokeless fuel and use wood fires carefully shrouded after darkness had fallen so that the fires would not be seen. Rations also were getting low as although we were in theory carrying twelve days', in practice it was more like ten which could be eked out to twelve if absolutely necessary.

It was a very useful day and having rested and planned, we now all looked forward to a good cooked meal before ambushing the next day. As planned we waited to well after darkness before we started cooking. Unfortunately not all the fires were properly shrouded and before long we heard the distant thud of mortars from our north followed by the crump of exploding bombs in the nearby swamp to our east. By the time the fires were doused two more salvoes of bombs had landed close by and Peter Little and I were obliged to eat our much awaited meal half cooked and up to our knees in water in a slit trench! At least we had slit trenches since I always insisted we dug them when we halted for the night; 'A' Company on the other hand did not and were now frantically digging themselves in, to the not entire dissatisfaction of Support Company.

Whilst gloomily speculating on this latest development the dim form of my orderly materialised to offer the scrapings from a Brylcream jar of lime chutney. This touch of domesticity whilst mortar bombs crashed around struck an incongruous yet reassuring note. For him the issue was simpler, his job was to keep his Sahib fed and looked after and a few mortar bombs weren't going to dissuade him!

This unfortunate incident weighed even further against our

already slim chances of success but Colonel Nick remained adamant that we continue as planned. His voice clear and steady over the radio gave us a confidence that the circumstances did not really justify.

The next day, a Saturday, we set off early, leaving behind about thirty men under the 'A' Company Sergeant Major to guard the base. My company led off with the Reconnaissance Platoon up in the lead. After about two hours march we reached a big bend in the river and having carried out a reconnaissance found an excellent ambush position for two companies. Len was content with my intended layout so we started to move into position.

Until this moment I had not realised how much longer it took to get two companies into an ambush than one and as our present luck would have it, just as the last platoon of 'A' Company was getting into position two big boats came up river. They were manned by civilians dressed similarly in white singlets and trousers. I was near enough to see the fear in their eyes as they sighted 'A' Company moving into position.

Three options flashed through my mind; stop the boats and capture the boatmen, kill the boatmen and sink the boats which were anyhow probably carrying Indonesian supplies, let the boats go on and move to yet another ambush position. The first two options needed really quick reaction and with my soldiers spread out in ambush positions speed was difficult. Perhaps in the end my own cumulative tiredness after months in the jungle and recurrent sickness blunted my reactions for I did nothing except weakly attempt to shift the burden onto Colonel Nick's shoulders by radioing back to him for guidance as to what to do next.

Colonel Nick's certainty that we should continue was now

weakening. This operation seemed fated not to succeed and the longer we stayed the more likely we were to be cut off and forced to fight at a considerable disadvantage. Logic and prudence demanded that we withdraw now and speedily. Then for some extraordinary reason which I didn't really understand myself, I found myself counselling one more try. Perhaps it was the frustration of impending failure after all the effort expended and chances missed or perhaps it was a streak of fatalism that prompted me to accept the inevitability of eventual battle on adverse terms.

Either way we agreed on one last try and so sending the companies back under their respective Seconds in Command, Len and I with a small protection party looked for another ambush position further up river. There were five boats that came up river during that long afternoon all crewed by sturdy boatmen in the same singlets and slacks. Len and I were convinced they were Indonesian soldiers dressed as civilians in order to avoid interception by us. Fortunately we heard them all well down river and thus avoided detection. Eventually as darkness was gathering we found an ideal ambush position; a long low thickly jungled ledge giving clear fields of fire for all our weapons and plenty of room for both companies. It was even bisected by a shallow stream which neatly split the ledge into two company positions.

We didn't reach camp until nightfall and even Len looked tired; captain of the Battalion football team and strong and supremely fit as he was. Then followed the requirement to plan and give out orders in order to cover every eventuality and finally to double check. That night there was no rum and little to eat but we consoled ourselves with the thought that we had found the best possible ambush position, although I personally doubted that any Indonesian soldier would be fool enough to come into it.

Looming large in all our plans was the strong possibility that the Indonesians would try and cut us off or attack the ambush from the rear, as had happened last time. As a result two strong platoons guarded the flanks of the ambush whilst in addition to the ten sick men in base there were a further twelve or so guarding it. The artillery fire plan was carefully tied into the plan and Captain 'Chalky' White our Artillery Officer seemed to have matters well tied up in that normal efficient way that all Gunners seem to have.

Our plans made there was now only the night between them and their realisation. As I lay in the darkness gazing up at the immensity of the jungle I felt so close in spirit to the patient Gurkhas sleeping under the same stars that some snippet of half forgotten Shakespeare returned:

'We few, we happy few, we band of brothers,
for he today that sheds his blood with me
shall be my brother. . .'

The next morning was dry, and far up high in the canopy of the jungle sunlight shafted through the branches. In the gloom below, a long line of Gurkhas, bandoliers of ammunition slung over their shoulders, trudged off towards the ambush position. They looked set, purposeful and menacing but for me they had a smile of confidence and comradeship; I hoped the future would show that I deserved it.

With great care we slunk into our ambush positions and arranged our weapons. Looking at the almost endless obscured olive green forms of the soldiers and thinking of the concentrated firepower of their weapons I could not conceive that any Indonesian force caught within the ambush could survive. The long shelving bank afforded no hiding places from the raking fire of our machine guns.

After about an hour and a half my Signaller got a message for me to go and see Len Lauderdale. Since any movement in the ambush was prohibited I queried this getting on to Len himself. He then told me that he had received a message from his Sergeant Major in charge of the base that his sentries had sighted the Indonesians closing in to attack . . . Our worst and long anticipated fears were realised; the Indonesians had known we were in the area and had searched for our base knowing it to be the most vulnerable and absolutely vital link in our operation. As I crawled through the undergrowth and muddy stream towards Len, my mind raced as to what we should do.

By the time I got to Len I knew the answer -- we must regain the initiative and throw the Indonesians off balance to give us time to get to the base before they attacked and overran it. Our only trump card was the 105 gun on the border; if this opened fire on Berdjonkong the Indonesians would hesitate; perhaps for long enough to let us get back. Len was only too happy to go along with this plan and we decided that as we approached the base we would split, Len going to his area in the north and Support Company to the south. We arranged for the gun to fire after ten minutes and then briefed the Platoon Commanders as quickly as possible on this complete change of plan.

As the first shell was fired we were on our way half walking, half running towards what we knew would be a confused and bloody encounter. All were seized by the strength of desperation, Machine Gunners swathed in ammunition belts, heavy GPMGs balanced on their shoulders, leapt from tussock to tussock in the shallow swamp. Our one aim was to get to the Indonesians before they took our base with its sick men, rations, medicine, back up radios etc.

As we neared the familiar low hill we spread out into skirmishing order and cautiously crept up on our position. Conscious of the danger of being fired on by our own men we kept a running commentary of our progress to them on the radio; then blessed relief -- we had made contact with our own men before the Indonesians attacked. In an instant our men were clambering into their slit trenches and aligning their weapons on the perimeter.

It was only then that the ghastly anti-climax became apparent. There were no enemy near the camp! The 'A' Company Sergeant Major heeding a report of a jumpy or inexperienced sentry had mistaken the changeover of his own base sentries for Indonesian scouts!

As I realised this I felt totally drained and temporarily beyond constructive thought apart from ordering the gun to stop firing. So much effort, so much re-planning, so much hope all dashed by an incompetent Warrant Officer! In my rage his kindness and companionship were forgotten, and also how easy it was in thick jungle to make such an error. Thankfully he was not in my company and I left Len to deal with him.

Sitting in silent anger I took stock of the situation. All surprise was lost, rations were nearly exhausted and the Indonesians would certainly soon be looking for us. It then occurred to me that perhaps we could turn this debacle to advantage.

If Len and 'A' Company left us some of their rations we could ambush the approaches to our camp from Berdjonkong so that when the Indonesians came looking for us, as inevitably they would, we could inflict a reverse on them.

However when we explained matters to Colonel Nick he would have none of it; I think he had now despaired of us ever achieving success and ordered us to return.

Slowly and disconsolately but not without a measure of relief we headed back through waist high swamp and torrential rain for the border. So difficult was the going that it took us three days to get back and a further day sitting on the LZ waiting for helicopters; unsuccessful companies seldom merited quick evacuation. John Parkes, our Adjutant, nevertheless took compassion and sent out a light helicopter with a case of rum.

Back at Lundu after shaving off my beard and showering I made my way to the old District Commissioner's house to explain matters to Colonel Nick, who was very understanding and apart from giving me a mild ticking off for firing the gun indiscriminately, had no hard words. On the credit side he hoisted in the fact that large numbers did not necessarily make for successful operations. Such was the nature of the country and the enemy that a single company formed the most effective striking force, albeit as part of a larger operation.

That rainy afternoon I sat in my room writing up the operational report, reading the pile of mail awaiting me and reflecting on our incredible good fortune that despite mistakes and bad luck we had all got out physically unscathed. I say physically because a day later the unfortunate 'A' Company Sergeant Major was on his way back to Nepal via Singapore on premature retirement. Colonel Nick had a short way with those whom he felt had failed the Regiment.

Chapter 9

15 NOVEMBER – 19 NOVEMBER 1965

As our time for handover to 42 Royal Marine Commando got to within a month I wondered whether we would be required to cross the border again. Certainly all the companies were rather looking over their shoulders to the preparations for their return back to Singapore. In our case particularly there were certain key personnel to be got back early for mortar and anti tank gun courses, although I was very reluctant to lose any of my experienced soldiers if we were needed for another 'Claret' operation.

However I wasn't left long in suspense for a couple of days later as we were seeing off John Masters, Colonel Nick warned me to be ready for a joint operation in 'C' Company's area to the south of the battalion sector in a few days' time. It was odd to be happily reminiscing with a convalescent John and at the same time be under orders for another 'Claret' operation.

John had been so much a part of all our operations that his very presence had become a talisman of success. Certainly our last operation without him had been far from successful and superstitiously I wondered if our luck had broken. John still looked thin and wasted from his scrub typhus. Amid cheers and waves from the company he climbed onto the old twin Pioneer plane and left Borneo. A part of me felt rather envious.

Next morning I found myself flying over to Bokah to plan the operation with the 'C' Company Commander, Major Geoffrey Ashley. Geoff was perhaps the most skilful of our Company Commanders. He planned in great detail and prior to every operation he carried out the most comprehensive reconnaissance. As a person he was a charming, slightly vague officer, distinguished but totally lacking in flamboyance. He and his lovely Dutch wife Cornelia were a delightful couple who managed to live a happy, highly cultivated life despite Geoff's continual absences in Borneo which must have been an immense strain so early in their married life.

Geoff had carried out one particularly successful operation which had used a boat ambush to lure out a strong Indonesian cut off attempt which in its turn was devastatingly ambushed by the bulk of 'C' Company, killing some thirty Indonesians. Rumour had it that the Brigadier flew to Bokah to congratulate Geoff who in his vague way had forgotten about the visit. In fury the Brigadier stormed off and despite his brilliant ambush Geoff received no recognition whatsoever.

'C' Company's base was as I should have expected; not only well defended militarily but made charming and civilized as well. Subsequently a combination of fresh coffee and different surroundings gave an almost carefree feeling which was certainly not warranted by the subject to be discussed.

As we drank our coffee Geoff unfolded his plan. In his modest way he described how, after a series of reconnaissance patrols, he had discovered the existence of two major enemy camps housing at least a company each on the far bank of the River Separan, a tributary of the sizeable River Khumba. He had noticed a lot of military boat movement on the Separan and suspected that if two ambushes could be laid the two camps would inevitably use the Separan to help each other out which should enable us to execute our classic double ambush manoeuvre.

The next day Geoff intended to carry out a confirmatory reconnaissance after which we would mount the operation on the 13th November. After a delicious lunch accompanied by cold Danish lager, I set off back to Lundu to get the company ready. I had great confidence in Geoff and was thus content to completely follow his plan.

My first task on getting back to Lundu was to endeavour to get some proper five thousand foot vertical air photos of the area in which I was to operate. In the end all I could get was the normal ten thousand foot verticals which gave very little information. These photos were taken by RAF Canberra photo Reconnaissance planes flying along the border and understandably they were reluctant to fly at five thousand feet for fear of ground fire. Nevertheless when they did so such air photos were quite invaluable and lack of them on this operation could have proved to be very adverse.

Although this was to be a two company operation 'C' Company would be four or five miles away so we were virtually operating independently. I preferred this as although there was not the strength conferred by larger numbers there was more flexibility in operation and less chance of being discovered.

That afternoon my new Second in Command had flown in from Singapore. I knew him well from our last operational tour in the Second Division of Borneo. He was a sound, very conscientious officer but lacked the intelligence and operational flair of Captain Surendraman. Also he found it difficult to come to terms with the much greater size and scope of the type of operation we were now undertaking. It followed that his continual advice for caution and reassessment whilst very well meant simply was not in accord with what was required.

The days that followed saw the by now familiar build up of the company for an operation. The testing of weapons on the jungle range, the practising of ambush tactics, the laying in of lightweight rations. Perhaps most important were the continual briefings so that every man understood his place in the column, his position in the ambush and his task on meeting with the enemy. This was particularly important at this time since many of the soldiers had changed and had not been in action before.

Now that John Masters had gone for good, we had a new Forward Observation Artillery Officer called Chris Mutton, a strong cheerful Lieutenant who had come to us under something of a cloud from Hong Kong. Together we pored over the air photos and tried to make some sense out of their universal impenetrability.

At this stage our battalion was more committed to the border war than at any other time. It was unusual for there to be more than one company in base with all the others across the border on 'Claret' operations. 'B' Company ambushing deep in Indonesia had sunk a motor launch with several senior Indonesian officers in it. They were commanded by Major Mike Joy a very experienced Commander who had carefully pieced together all the invaluable SAS reports on this particular stretch of river. 'D' Company too under the indefatigable Piers Erskine Tulloch operating on another stretch of river had sunk a large diesel barge with about twenty soldiers in it.

With such continuous losses one could not help but wonder how the Indonesians would react. There really seemed little they could do to regain the initiative short of mounting a major attack themselves.

So the wheels ground on, news of operations percolated in, some successful some not; yet in Lundu we seemed amazingly cut off from the jungle war, the sun peacefully setting over the river and the dim lights of the bazaar flickering invitingly of an evening.

As planned the company flew out to 'C' Company's base at Bokah and by midday of the 14th of November we were all there. Then followed a day of final checks, the test firing of weapons and the final coordination of our plans with 'C' Company.

The plan was for one or other of the companies to spring the ambush when both were in position whilst the other one ambushed the expected boatloads of Indonesians coming to deal with the ambush. Geoff warned me of the steep hills and difficult going as well as a number of rivers to cross before we got to the Separan.

That evening, lit by the gentle light of paraffin lamps, Geoff, myself and Captain David Thomas, the Battalion Signals Officer, sat with our Gurkha officers and enjoyed a civilized meal, the last for several days to come. David Thomas was an old friend of mine and since he was to take over the company when I went on leave after this operational tour it had seemed sensible for him to accompany us as an observer. Like Geoffrey and Cornelia, David and his attractive clever wife Joanna were very close friends so it was an evening of great warmth and comradeship.

I had been most impressed during the course of the afternoon with 'C' Company's arrangements. Geoff had rigorously cut down the overall weight carried by each man. During operations he forbade his men any cooking thus reducing the weight of chemical fuel to be carried.

At night 'C' Company just kept marching until dusk fell when they rolled up for the night in groundsheets. This avoided any time spent in making base or the give-away noise of chopping.

I reflected nevertheless that while these methods suited 'C' Company in their dry hilly area, in our habitual swamp the deprivation of hot food and a dry sleep would render our men unfit for combat in a very short space of time.

That night I slept deeply in the comfortable bunk that Geoff kept for visitors.

The next morning dawned misty with a light rain and as I sipped the hot tea my orderly had brought I wondered what fate would hold for us beyond the mist shrouded ridge that marked the border.

Unusually I had decided not to go with the company on their four mile march to the border. I was still convalescent after yet another bout of fever and felt it pointless to exhaust myself by climbing the one thousand foot high border range of hills when I could fly in later on the helicopter bringing the last of the mortar and gun ammunition and the company packs.

I watched the company set off, confident and purposeful as ever on what was to be our last 'Claret' operation. I would join them by last light for a final briefing before we set off next morning into Kalimantan.

After they had left I sat down on Geoff's little verandah and looked out over the hills with a certain feeling of 'deja vu'. My mind raced over all those other occasions when we had set out for Indonesia over the last two years, on a variety of cross border operations.

At about 10.00 in the morning a call came from John Parkes at Lundu telling us that our plans might have to be changed if we found the Separan to be in flood in which case we should cross it and ambush further inland on a land supply route. The fact that I had not gone with the company was fortuitous as I was able to discuss this latest development with Geoff who was also going to join his company that evening.

He was the only person who could talk with any authority on this stretch of the Separan having reconnoitred it extensively a month ago. He warned me it would be a major obstacle to get across and an even worse one over which to withdraw in a hurry and under fire. Nevertheless he felt confident that there would be a main track further inland linking the various enemy camps together.

After a light lunch we started getting our stuff together and after a final talk set off by helicopter for our respective companies.

On arrival with Support Company I found that our Mortar Fire Controller had ruptured his appendix climbing up the border ridge. Fortunately we were able to bring in a replacement on the last of the helicopters delivering ammunition, flying the casualty back to Kuching hospital.

Before the light started to fail I climbed up the high lookout tower that 'C' Company had constructed from where I had a good view of the country we had to cross in the next few days. The area was covered with thick jungle, a deep valley in front of us rising to a high ridge upon the crest of which I could see little sugar loaf shaped rock formations.

After giving out orders for the next day's march I went round the company talking to the soldiers. They all seemed cheerful and confident; even the new Mortar Fire Controller plucked out of the comparative calm of Lundu with barely time to fill his pack.

That night it was very cool on our high ridge and I was glad of my blanket.

The next morning after tea and 'dog' biscuits we set off down the steep slope to the valley below making good speed through the dry clear jungle. After about an hour we came to a quite lovely glade with a stream tumbling down it to a sunlit pool. The water was cool and clear and small fish darted thither and thence, it was altogether an idyllic picture.

As we descended steeply to the valley bottom I slipped and fell down the sheer side of a rocky gorge and onto the rocks below. Fortunately I fell flat on my back and was protected by my heavy pack -- the first time I had blessed it! Although bruised and shaken no bones were broken and I could still walk, which was all that was required.

At midday we stopped in the valley which was thickly forested with primary jungle and ate our sardines and biscuits whilst I gave Battalion HQ a quick resume on our progress, to be passed on to 'C' Company with whom we were not in direct radio contact.

That afternoon we pushed on through the valley, interspersed by small steep hills of the sugar loaf type I had seen from the lookout tower. They seemed to be limestone outcrops. At about 4.00 we came across a quite large deep river which my air photograph did not show. Geoff had warned me that the valley was intersected with rivers and this one was certainly a considerable obstacle. Leaving the imperturbable Lieutenant Nandaraj to work out how to bridge the river I took the rest of the company to a nearby ridge to make camp.

That evening looking at the map and air photo I calculated that we had covered over three miles which was excellent going and should bring us close to the Separan after the next morning's march.

At first light on the 17th of November we set off to the river and on arrival I placed the Reconnaissance Platoon up stream of the bridging site and the Anti Tanks down stream with orders to open fire on any enemy boats coming into the bridging site and to give us as early warning as possible of any civilian boats. Once the flank guards were in position Lieutenant Nandaraj started work. First a young Gurkha Pioneer climbed to the topmost branches of a thick, straight and smooth barked tree selected by Nandaraj as being just the right distance from the river. Once at the top of the tree he lashed on the rope tied to his waist and climbed down. It was then quietly sawn through at the base with a folding saw and then like a ship's derrick it was dropped over the river. Another young Pioneer then unconcernedly walked over the fallen tree to the other side of the river carrying two ropes which he lashed tight as handrails. Done under the skilled direction of Nandaraj it looked very easy but in other hands I had seen it go very awry.

The company then filed over the deep and turgid river and finally the Pioneers took in the ropes, hauled the tree over the river and hid it, covering the sawn wood with mud.

No sooner had I finished mentally congratulating myself on the smoothness of the river crossing than the leading scout signalled yet another river. Going forward to investigate I found a much larger river, which I thought must show up on the air photos but did not.

The first crossing had obviously gone too smoothly as this time not only was there a wider river and less suitable trees for felling, but also drama. Just as Nandaraj's Pioneers were lowering their bridge the Anti Tanks heard the sound of a motor launch downstream. Frantically the Pioneers hauled the tree back up and we waited with bated breath. The launch appeared to take the river we had just crossed so we presumed a junction a few hundred yards downstream. Again it was not shown on the air photo which was proving of very limited assistance, in fact, its main use was under my groundsheet to keep me dry at night.

It was midday before we had the river behind us and the company were in a defensive perimeter on top of a low hill prior to sending our patrols to find the main river.

After the usual dog biscuits and sardines I sent out three patrols on different bearings to look for the main river which should have been by now fairly close. I decided to take one of the patrols myself as it would save me time later deciding whether to ambush the river or cross it.

As I munched my biscuits I looked over to where Lieutenant Chris Mutton the Artillery Forward Observation Officer was sitting. His conduct on the operation so far had impressed me very favourably. One of his two British Signallers was physically not up to the rigours of this type of operation and had started to lag behind so Chris was now carrying his Signaller's radio set as well as the bulk of both their rations. The Gurkhas had already taken greatly to him and called him 'Jhandiwalla Sahib' which means 'Signals-Sir' because he was carrying his own radio set! He was soon to prove his worth.

After swilling down the last of my biscuits with the tepid, chlorinated water from my bottle I set off with eight men from the Reconnaissance Platoon to find the river whilst patrols from the Anti Tanks and Pioneers set off on the same task on different bearings.

The going on our bearing was very difficult with a steep limestone escarpment to negotiate and yet another river which whilst clearly not the main one constituted a considerable brake on progress. Bereft of Nandaraj and his Pioneers we were reduced to lashing a long bamboo to a rock and then wading and swimming the rest. Thankfully our packs were with the rest of the company on the hill so movement was much easier.

After about another half mile or so the leading scout gave the signal for river and since the area was mossy and damp I reckoned that this was the main one. Just as I was on my way forward we heard the even clatter of an approaching helicopter. Under the jungle canopy we couldn't see anything but as the helicopter came overhead a heavy calibre machine gun opened fire from what seemed immediately in front of us. Using the radio set I asked Captain Minbahadur if he had seen anything from the top of the hill. He hadn't but far back on the border ridge the radio relay station had seen one of our own Whirlwind helicopters fly over the border, proceed into Indonesia and then having been hit by ground fire fly off trailing smoke.

Having joined my leading Scout at what was clearly the main river I could now hear the sound of excited Indonesian voices from the jungle on the other side. Clearly we had hit the river plumb opposite one of their bases to which the unfortunate helicopter had alerted us. What sounded like a 12.7mm heavy machine gun fired a further burst and then fell silent. Clearly it was no good contemplating crossing the river in this area and since it seemed to be flowing far too fast to be navigable and therefore to ambush, there didn't seem much point in staying any longer especially as I couldn't contact Battalion HQ direct from our patrol radio set.

Accordingly we returned and on arrival back with the company, wet and tired, I composed my thoughts over a welcome cup of tea and then spoke to John Parkes on the radio. Since the RAF had denied losing one of their helicopters John naturally thought the Indonesians had shot down one of their own. We were quickly able to put him right as the radio rebroadcast station had clearly seen the RAF roundels and identified it as a Whirlwind. Whilst Battalion HQ deliberated on what action to take about the shot down helicopter I had a chance to talk to the other two Patrol Commanders one of whom was Lieutenant Nandaraj. He had found a possible place to cross south of where I had been. Apparently a huge tree had fallen two thirds across the very fast flowing river and he felt he might be able to develop it into a bridge. He too felt the river was flowing far too fast to carry any river traffic and therefore to be worth ambushing. Unfortunately although the surrounding hinterland was mainly primary jungle the area around the possible bridging point was low lying rather open scrub and secondary jungle which had probably been cultivated two or three years before for rice or maize. The other Patrol Commander had been unable to find any suitable area to ambush or cross.

I felt uneasy sitting on top of our rather obvious hill and told Captain Minbahadur to get the company packed up prior to making base nearer the area that Nandaraj had reconnoitred. Just as we were setting off John Parkes came up on the radio again instructing me to continue as planned

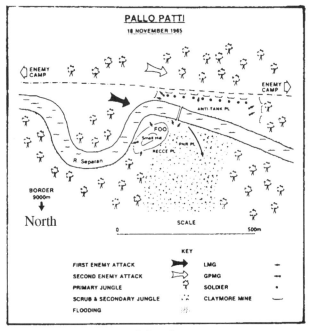

Map 6

but telling me also that a large scale rescue operation was shortly to be attempted to recover the pilot and passenger of the stricken helicopter. I was able to pass on to him the latest news from our watchful observation post that the helicopter had crashed to the east of a known Indonesian base at a place called Kindau which was well to the south of where I was intending to ambush.

It was now getting rather late and by the time we reached the edge of the cleared area of cultivation described by Nandaraj after his reconnaissance the light was already fading. Leaving Captain Minbahadur with the main body of the company to make base and forbidding any cooking I set off with the Platoon Commanders to reconnoitre the river.

In the half light we stumbled over the blackened boles of felled and burnt trees, the site of previous maize cultivation, until finally we reached the river.

It was a formidable obstacle about eighty feet wide, deep, turgid and very fast flowing. It was a far larger river than we had ever attempted to cross but by great good fortune a large tree had fallen over the deepest channel and its highest branches lay in a jumble only twenty feet or so from the other side.

It was clear to me that the river was flowing too fast for any boat traffic and so we would have to cross it and search for the big inter-connecting track we had been told about in our initial briefing. Could Lieutenant Nandaraj construct a bridge based on the fallen tree which I uneasily noted continually shifted in the torrent? This fine officer gave no reply for a good fifteen minutes whilst he examined the tree and the bank meticulously. Finally he came back in the affirmative providing I could give him an hour and a half the next morning before we crossed.

Stumbling back through the darkness I became even more convinced that a river ambush would be quite fruitless. The Separan was in spate and if we were to achieve our aim we had to ambush on the other side on the inter-connecting track if one really existed since there was no sign of it on the quite useless air photos. This would mean that if we suffered casualties we would have to get them over three large rivers before getting back to the border. It wasn't really a thought worth pondering.

I briefly considered giving the responsibility for crossing to Colonel Nick but by the time I got back to the company I had decided to cross knowing that was what he would have wanted. The main lesson from our last operation was to seize opportunity as soon as it presented itself and I felt the fallen tree offered just such an opportunity.

On arrival at the base I gave a warning order to the company to be ready to move an hour before dawn and then sat down to work out my plan for crossing the river with the least risk. As I wrote in the pinprick glow of a shaded torch Captain Minbahadur my company Second in Command came and sitting down endeavoured to dissuade me from crossing the river. I tried to reassure him at the same time longing for that close relationship of understanding and utter support that I had enjoyed with Surendraman.

It was not until about 10.00 that I was ready to give out orders. The rain pattered down on the dark shapes of the soldiers huddled under their poncho capes as the Platoon Commanders materialised in the gloom to hear the plan and their part in it.

In essence the plan was to move out at 5.00 in the morning which was an hour or so before dawn and placing the Reconnaissance Platoon on a small hill to the south of the fallen tree and the Anti Tank Platoon to the north for the Pioneers then to set to work turning it into a bridge. What took the time of course was not the simple plan but all the contingency arrangements necessary to ensure an immediate reaction should the Indonesians turn up whilst the Pioneers were suspended as it were between heaven and the river. Since the Indonesians could conceivably approach from any direction the variables were almost limitless and all had to be considered as the Indonesians would be thoroughly stirred up by the helicopter affair and thus their patrols could appear at any time. In the nightly SITREP back to Battalion HQ I limited myself to 'Nothing to report' since there was nothing to report -- yet!

Having chewed my dry biscuits I turned over and went to sleep only to be woken by Captain Minbahadur and Lieutenant Nandaraj both imploring me to ambush the river as in their opinion to cross it would be to invite disaster. This was a complete turnabout for Nandaraj and I guessed Minbahadur had been getting at him. I explained that we had been ordered to ambush the enemy and that was what we were going to do and since the river was unnavigable we must find the interconnecting path between the enemy camps. Nevertheless after they had gone I began to have doubts myself as we were certainly putting ourselves in a potentially very dangerous situation.

I awoke stiff and pained in my back from where I had fallen on the first day -- it seemed an age ago. Without the warmth of a magic brew of tea (because of our probable close proximity to the enemy) pulling on filthy wet clothes was more than usually unpleasant. Our camp of the night had been of the most rudimentary and in a few minutes all was ready and the men, appearing as areas of increased darkness in the gloom, crouched by their weapons awaiting the signal to move out. How I admired them for their stoic professionalism so liberally spiced with warmth and humour! Soon came the signal that the sentries were stood down and so the long column wound its way out as on what seemed a lifetime of similar occasions. That strange mixture of fear and excitement vied with intense relief that the final phase had now started, despite all the previous doubts.

As we neared the river a thrill of pride ran through me transcending chill clothes, semi-darkness and swirling mist and rain for there in total silence my plan was given substance: the Reconnaissance Platoon with Chris Mutton, our imperturbable Artillery Officer, silently and purposefully occupied their hill, the Anti Tanks fanned out in the gloom to the defence positions just inside the jungle to the north (see sketch) whilst Nandaraj and his Pioneers, divesting themselves of packs and equipment, set about their task. Soon came the muffled sound of folding saws as supports, extra tree trunks and vines were assembled.

Leaving Nandaraj I went to the Reconnaissance Platoon hill and watched the slow approach of dawn over the dark immensity of the jungle. Gradually the rain abated and on the horizon a livid orange crack opened in the vault of heaven slowly widening and brightening until the glistening canopy of the jungle was lit by it. Below from the swirling torrent of the river half hidden in mist came the muffled sounds of piles being driven into the river bed. I could not help but think what a perfect setting it would have made for the anvil chorus from 'Il Trovatore'!

Exactly an hour after we had started, Lieutenant Nandaraj crested the hill. 'Tyari Chha'; it was ready for crossing! I directed the Anti Tank Platoon to cross to form a bridgehead on the other side. As I went across with them I wondered at the ingenuity of Nandaraj's men in bridging the river. The tree still moved with the current and Pioneers stripped to their briefs struggled in the water lashing the trunk to the piles they had driven in. Where the fallen tree ended Nandaraj had lashed on another complete tree to bridge the remaining twenty feet of swirling water. Here the rickety bridge was very hazardous as the main tree was slightly under water and slippery; so for a fully laden man it would be a trial, but for a wounded man being carried it would be a nightmare.

We had barely gone a hundred yards in the thick jungle on the other side when the signal came back for 'track'. Going forward I found that we had arrived at the main enemy lateral route between camps. I could tell this from the telegraph wire tacked above the track on trees it being enemy custom to run their telephone wire along tracks linking two bases together. The soft ground showed the recent imprint of Indonesian army boots.

My mind raced over how best to exploit this good fortune as I reconnoitred the track. Time was of the essence as Indonesian troops could soon be using it. The area itself although not ideal for ambush offered a good killing area to the west and a safe flank to the east since the path west ran along the river. This meant that as far as the eastern approach was concerned we would not be outflanked, always the biggest threat to an ambush. Lieutenant Deoparsad, the Commander of the Anti Tanks, was nothing if not intelligent and he quickly absorbed my plan for the layout of the ambush which I had already decided would be carried out by his platoon as it was on the spot. Leaving him to get his ambush in position I hastened back across the bridge to brief the others.

The Reconnaissance Platoon I left on the hill where they had a superb view of the rear and flanks of the ambush and the bridge, for the same reason I left Chris Mutton with them to control his guns from this vantage point. His task was to silence enemy mortars as soon as they fired, quite a tall order since he had only a vague idea where they might be. I detached four men including a Light Machine Gunner to guard the ambush end of our vital bridge. The Pioneers I left to guard all the other approaches to their bridge and to continue to work on it to make it as stable as possible since it was literally our lifeline. This done I told Nandaraj to send back a message to Captain Minbahadur and his firm base party as to what was happening whilst I gave Battalion HQ our rough ambush position. Then taking my orderly, Signaller and M79 Grenadier (a taciturn young Gurkha called Lalbahadur who operated our only M79 grenade launcher) I set off to command the ambush.

On arrival I found that Lieutenant Deoparsad had done well and apart from one or two slight alterations I left the ambush as he had laid it out.

As we took up our positions I checked my watch. It was 9.45, nearly four hours had passed in what seemed the space of a few minutes.

The sun was now high in the sky, its warmth penetrating the jungle canopy so that little clouds of vapour rose from the wet clothes of the ambushers. As I looked down the line of immobile figures with dark faces inscrutably searching the path I felt that at least all that was possible to carry out our mission had been done. To the west of the ambush two GPMG (medium machine guns) commanded the killing area with another two LMG (light machine guns) to the east and one more in the centre whilst eleven Claymore mines covered the whole length of the path. I had given orders that the minimum target would be five men as to engage fewer would not be a worthwhile result after all the effort of the last few days.

I now became aware of intense hunger for apart from a packet of biscuits last night I had eaten nothing since the previous midday's sardines. I thus gingerly edged out a pack of hard tack biscuits from my pouch and giving one to my M79 Grenadier next to me was about to eat them when I heard voices followed by the signal for enemy, 'thumbs down'. Moments later three Indonesian soldiers walked by talking desultorily. One had his Armalite rifle balanced on his shoulder. They were so close that I could hear the sucking of their boots in the mud. The M79 Grenadier next to me sat immobile with my biscuit still clenched between his teeth!

For a ghastly moment I had visions of a complete Indonesian company all moving along in threes and never being fired at! I need not have worried for seconds later another group of six with a machine gun passed through followed by a long heavily armed column. Lieutenant Deoparsad with great prescience allowed the main body of the enemy to get well into the killing area before opening fire with his two GPMGs and detonating his Claymores followed by the concerted fire of the rest of the ambush. It seemed a perfectly executed operation. After a short pause the stunned Indonesians started to react. Never lacking in courage they counter-attacked to our east supported by mortar fire. As we had thought their outflanking tactics were negated by the river and the accurate fire of the ambush. Chris Mutton's guns were now firing from the border with commendable accuracy; the crump of their shells comfortingly protective.

I now did one of the more stupid things of my life. Remembering the Brigadier's directive to verify casualty claims I determined to count as many enemy dead as I could and so crawled out onto the path followed by a rather perplexed orderly. I counted eleven lying on or near the path in pathetic rag doll attitudes when a shout from my orderly warned me of an approaching enemy attack towards the centre of the ambush. One Indonesian soldier came to rest behind a branch directly in front of me and only after I had fired repeatedly at him did I realise that he was already dead before reaching the ground.

Lieutenant (QGO) Nandaraj Gurung *(right)* and his Platoon Sergeant
Imansing Gurung
*… I saw Nandaraj's pioneers ready with their kurkris to cut the
lashing holding the bridge*

This counter attack again came to nothing and my most
vivid memory was of Lalbahadur our M79 Grenadier
speeding the parting guest with our entire allotment of M79
grenades.

I realised I must seize this lull to withdraw the ambush
before a properly coordinated attack came in. From the
shouted orders of the enemy and their intensifying mortar
fire I realised this could not be long delayed. Accordingly
the eastern ambush group withdrew dragging a young Lance
Corporal hit in the face by a mortar fragment. At the same
time I became aware that my right hand was bleeding
profusely hit either by a mortar fragment or Claymore mine
back-blast.

On two occasions Chris Mutton's guns silenced the enemy mortars but each time they started up again dropping their bombs all around us. Additionally a 12.7 heavy machine gun was now thudding away; fortunately well over our heads.

It seemed to take an age for both the western and eastern groups to get clear and it was with great relief when the signal came for our remaining centre group to cross. I was glad to find the stout Sergeant Chabilal, Platoon Commander of the Reconnaissance Platoon, was himself at the bridgehead superintending things. Mortar bombs fell all round the bridge which seemed more unsteady than ever; I saw Nandaraj's Pioneers ready with their kukris to cut the lashings holding the bridge once we were all across.

Every impulse was for getting out as fast as we could before the next counter attack came in but to cut the bridge loose before every single man was accounted for could be to sign a man's death warrant and bring dishonour upon us all. Having been through all this once before there could be no mistake this time. So as Sergeant Chabilal shepherded his bridge protection party over the swirling river with agonising slowness, I had Lieutenant Deoparsad check all his men again.

We were complete; sharp kukris cut the lashings and the bridge lurched drunkenly and then with a crashing and rending broke loose and went down river. I think British soldiers would have probably cheered but the Gurkhas merely resheathed their Kukris and moved off.

I realised that after this reverse the Indonesians would attempt to cut us off so as soon as we reached our firm base I took ten minutes or so to work out a withdrawal route that would confuse the Indonesians. Working with me was Chris Mutton whose guns would cover us and which were now pounding our old ambush position. Chris was a tower of strength; nothing depressed him and any setback left him laughing. He was still carrying his signaller's radio set.

To this end we set off due east only veering to the north after about an hour. Punctuating the afternoon were the signal shots of the pursuing Indonesians but although they continued well into nightfall each minute of our march lessened the likelihood of them intercepting us. From time to time Chris Mutton brought his guns into action and I seized one of these opportunities to tell Colonel Nick of our success; he was elated. It transpired that 'C' Company despite all their skill had been most unluckily discovered by the Indonesians and had had to turn back, which made our success even more welcome.

That night we dug in really well, having crossed the second of the main rivers. After ranging-in Chris' s guns we felt secure enough to cook up a decent meal; the first the company had eaten for two days. The wounded NCO had received a fragment through one cheek and out the other with no damage apart from loss of blood. In my case the fragment had gone through a finger causing no real damage. Our luck had again held.

The Gurkha medical orderly was a great character called Manbahadur, who besides patching us up quite expertly, produced a new unopened bottle of Gordon's Gin which he announced he had no intention of carrying further. The company therefore lightened his load and all felt the better for it.

The next day we marched fast in the well drained hill jungle, crossed the last big river without incident and by midday were able to tell Battalion HQ that we were an hour from the border landing zone.

Patrol crossing a clearing
Photo: N.T. Corbett

A measure of our success was that two Whirlwinds were actually on the ground waiting for us with a third buzzing around preparatory to landing. This was glory!

As we slogged up the final steep border ridge I realised that this was the last time I would take Support Company across the border to action. The Royal Marine Commando advance party had already arrived and I had been designated Battalion baggage officer for the move back! I would then go on six months UK leave which I knew I needed if only to get rid of my recurring fever. Before I went I intended to go to Nepal for two months to see what sort of environment raised these unique soldiers.

Perhaps they were at their most impressive now, brown skins bleached yellow by jungle gloom and wet clothes in shreds from thorn and branch yet each man carried himself

L/Cpl Resambahadur Thapa MM gets his
machine gun aboard

'Goodbye Lundu!' We hand over to the Marines

like a warrior and every weapon was clean and lightly oiled.

By lunchtime I was in Colonel Nick's den explaining the operation; he had been on Lundu landing zone to meet us.

Spread out in front of us were the air photos that I had so needed; five thousand foot verticals which showed every river, hill and clearing. By looking at them I could see clearly that our ambush position was a bare fifty yards from one of the enemy main bases; no wonder they were surprised! Thinking about it later I came to the sombre conclusion that somewhere in that column we ambushed were probably the captured pilot and passengers of the downed helicopter. No doubt the Indonesians killed them, for they were never seen again. I had no proof that this was so but such a large troop movement must have had some purpose, and escorting prisoners was a likely one.

After showering and having my hand dressed I went over to visit the company; already the first games of chance were in progress to celebrate the annual Nepali gambling festival of Diwali. I reflected that the successful conclusion of our last operation represented a fortunate ending to one of the company's biggest gambles. The sad stake was fifteen or so dead Indonesians.

Chapter 10

Thus had ended our final 'Claret' operation and apart from a local operation against Communist terrorists which yielded important but negative information we did not go into the jungle again in 1st Division of Borneo. The leeches would sway their grotesque gavotte towards somebody else's blood and other columns would mark the decaying traces of our island resting places in the depressing immensity of the swamp. A few scarred trees and empty cartridge cases would be our epitaph.

Soon our days were taken up with packing and getting ready to hand over to the Marines. As part of the handover I had to brief the Marine Company Commander taking over my operational area on both sides of the border. He turned out to be a particularly fierce ginger-headed Major who had been the terror of our lives during our Platoon Commanders course at Warminster some three years back. He did not recognise me, indeed there was no reason why he should, given that hundreds of students must have passed through his hands. On the other hand I recognised him well and it was not without a certain sense of satisfaction that I saw him plainly apprehensive at the type of operation which he would soon be called upon to undertake!

Whilst we had finished operations other companies were involved until literally the last day. 'A' and 'D' Companies under Piers Erskine-Tulloch with Chris Mutton as his FOO got the battle he wanted. Having been shadowed by an Indonesian company on his way to ambush he was attacked while resting. After a fierce and confused battle the Indonesians were finally driven off by well directed small arms fire from the two companies as well as superbly coordinated artillery fire brought down by Chris Mutton.

Later in a separate operation, 'A' Company, commanded by Len Lauderdale, was attacked whilst moving into ambush and after a hard fight involving several casualties extricated itself successfully. The Marine officer who had gone with them to see the area ended up by carrying a severely wounded Gurkha all the way back to the border.

A couple of days before we were to leave Brigadier Cheyne visited us and talked to the whole of Support Company from an impromptu stage of ammunition boxes. I suppose his disagreements with Colonel Nick inevitably influenced me against him as did his rather simplistic approach when debriefing me on 'Operation Hell Fire'. On this occasion however I admired the soldierly way he congratulated the soldiers. Since few spoke English I doubt they understood the words but they greatly appreciated the feelings expressed. He then went on to speak to every other company in the same vein. Given the pressure of his job this was a fine gesture to have made.

On leaving Borneo our handover to the Marines only took a day, the helicopters from the carrier HMS Albion shuttling them in and us out at an amazing rate until two collided killing twelve; a very sad moment. Even during our return to peaceful Singapore there was still to be drama. The passage should only have taken two days but in the event took four. Later I discovered why; the Prime Minister (Wilson), despairing of a peaceful agreement for the future of Rhodesia started considering military options. A battle-experienced Gurkha battalion already embarked with all its weapons and equipment was obviously a factor to be considered and so we turned towards the Indian Ocean until wiser counsels prevailed. If he had known how sea sick the Gurkhas became perhaps he wouldn't have delayed us!

When we docked at Singapore the Regimental Band struck up on the jetty and wives and girl friends waved. The Brigadier commanding Singapore Base Area strode up the gang plank and grasping the Senior Company Commander's hand was heard to say, 'Glad to see you back Piers, now we can get down to some proper training!'

Many of our splendid soldiers had soon to leave as the Brigade of Gurkhas was cut by over half once Confrontation had ended. When I returned back as Adjutant to the Battalion after leave it was my distasteful duty to send many fine men away on enforced redundancy after all we had been through together. However much I explained, they never really understood why I, of all people, should do this to them. Sometimes after long exhausting sessions with them I returned to my room in the Mess totally disillusioned with the system which, in its unseemly haste to dispense with those that had helped win Confrontation, affronted human dignity to such an extent.

Thankfully not all had to go and some of the best were saved. Captain Surendraman became Gurkha Major of the Battalion, the highest post for a Gurkha officer and Nandaraj after him. Gallant Reshambahadur who held the hill alone on Hell Fire became a Gurkha Major and Birbahadur who rallied the right flank on the same operation became a Captain. The Sergeant Major saved from death in the swamp recovered with only a slight limp and whilst in hospital blamed the company for deserting him. Western Gurkhas are slow to anger but when Support Company heard of this and remembering their efforts and especially those of John Masters they would have none of him and shortly after he joined the stream of redundant soldiers returning to Nepal. John himself reached high rank in the New Zealand army still keeping his close ties with the 2nd Gurkhas who made him a lifetime Honorary Member of their Regimental Association. The little Assault Pioneer, Hariprasad, who saved my bacon whilst we were searching for the Sergeant Major was made a Lance Corporal but then had to join those going on redundancy; thankfully it was not I who had to send him.

Of the British officers John Parkes and Peter Little (who had accompanied us on our abortive operation, Monsoon Drain), both commanded 2nd Gurkha Battalions whilst Norman Corbett our Intelligence Officer inherited wide acres in Wales and went off to farm them.

Johnny Lawes went on to command the Battalion with great success and it was my privilege to serve him again as a Company Commander. Piers then became Battalion Second in Command so the close family and fabric of the Regiment continued. David Thomas and Geoff Ashley both sadly left for successful careers outside the army, as did Len Lauderdale with whom Support Company had worked so closely and whose company had seen so much action.

So finally, to Colonel Nick Neill who guided our fortunes. The day he went off in a helicopter to rescue our wounded Sergeant Major from the swamp spelt the limit of his advancement. A more compromising man might still have made his peace with the Brigadier, but not Colonel Nick. For a while his career continued and after being promoted he went off to command the Gurkha Training Centre in Northern Malaya, but in the end it led to nothing and rather than drift into military obscurity far from the soldiers who were his life, he left the army. Now he can be seen walking the Cornish Devon borders, gun in hand and dog to heel. In the evenings he returns to his immaculate cottage and to the collected mementos of a fighting soldier's career, looked after and cherished by his wife. Not for him the subtle manoeuvrings inherent in a peacetime army. When the fighting ended, he hung up his sword and left, honoured to the end.

Finally to turn to the Gurkhas who bore the brunt of Confrontation. I believe that the Borneo war saw them at the peak of their operational effectiveness. The Brigade as such had hardly been out of action since the ending of World War 2. First in the internecine struggles in India during partition, then in Hanoi restoring the French administration and finally the twelve or so years of the Malayan emergency. When the Brunei revolt came in 1962 the ten Gurkha battalions were as finely tuned instruments of jungle warfare as could be envisaged. Their long and glorious history gave them immense pride in themselves and confidence; whilst the harsh environment of remote Nepal hill villages and farms bred in the soldiers toughness and self reliance to a high degree. In retrospect it is difficult to envisage such a successful conclusion to the three year Confrontation without the Brigade of Gurkhas but with them ultimate victory could not be long denied.

The extent of their achievements in Borneo was never

really understood back home or in GHQ in Singapore. This was mainly because of the utter secrecy in which 'Claret' operations were shrouded. Even the citations for bravery were carefully worded to give the impression that the actions took place 'on the border'. It follows that what seemed a courageous action on our own territory was doubly so five or so miles inside Indonesia.

Whatever we felt at the time, as jungle conflicts go the Borneo Confrontation was not an intense one when compared to Vietnam or the Burma campaign in the last war. But it was a most skilfully planned and executed one which produced ideas and tactics that subsequently became blueprints for the Australians in Vietnam. Unfortunately the Americans never seriously attempted to adopt such tactics and suffered very heavy casualties as a result.

Politically it was probably unique and could only have been waged in the way it was in a very undeveloped part of the world. Its success on the other hand was a military one. Long before Sockarno was toppled the Indonesian army had lost the initiative. This does not mean it was not capable of the occasional spectacular such as the storming of the Parachute Regiment base at Plaman Mapu. Rather it meant that in the daily routine of low level conflict such as this book describes the Indonesians were losing at their own game. Realising that they would be worsted in high level conflict they had opted for a massive guerilla campaign where their superior numbers should have told. Despite initial successes they failed; not through a lack of courage or perseverance but more because of poor leadership and shaky logistic support.

Oddly enough, whilst holidaying in Bali a year or so after Confrontation I chanced to talk to an Indonesian officer who

Men of Support Company

... Whatever face I see in the final ember is stamped with the same qualities; loyalty, courage, resource and humour ...

had been on the other side of the border. To him the issue was quite clear: we had raided into Indonesia regularly and just as regularly had been driven off so they had won. This struck me as a very soldierly explanation!

As I said at the beginning, this is a personal account and so necessarily painted on a small canvas. Sometimes on a winter's evening sitting in the light of the fire's glowing embers that canvas springs to life. Then again I see the gallant Resam covering our withdrawal or the patient scouts back-tracking John Master's trail. Time seems to stop still on these occasions and middle aged men living in Nepal are transported back to their youth and strength. Again they fight the current of the rushing Separan or marching in their long patient column set off on yet another hazardous mission. Whatever face I see in the final embers is always stamped with the same qualities: loyalty, courage, resource and humour.